SOME AMERICANS ABROAD

by the same author

SENSIBILITY AND SENSE

SOME
AMERICANS
ABROAD

RICHARD NELSON

faber and faber

LONDON · BOSTON

First published in 1989
by Faber and Faber Ltd
3 Queen Square London WCIN 3AU

A CIP record for this book is available from the British Library

Printed in the United States of America

Quality Printing and Binding by:
Berryville Graphics
P.O. Box 272
Berryville, VA 22611 U.S.A.

For Colin Chambers and Frank Pike

CHARACTERS

JOE TAYLOR, thirty-eight, recently appointed Chairman of the English Department
KATIE TAYLOR, his daughter, eighteen, attends the College
PHILIP BROWN, thirty-seven, a Professor of English
FRANKIE LEWIS, forty-one, an Associate Professor of English
ORSON BALDWIN, late sixties, retired Chairman of the English Department
HARRIET BALDWIN, his wife, sixties
HENRY McNEIL, thirty-five, Assistant Professor of English
BETTY McNEIL, his wife, thirty-six
DONNA SILLIMAN, twenty, a student at the College
JOANNE SMITH, twenty-six, a graduate of the College
AN AMERICAN, forties

All the characters are American.

Some Americans Abroad is set at approximately the present time in various locations in England. Each scene has a title—the location of the scene—which should be projected moments before the scene begins.

This play was commissioned by the Royal Shakespeare Company.

Some Americans Abroad was first performed at The Pit, London, on 19 July 1989.

ACT ONE

ACT ONE

ACT ONE

SCENE 1

Projection: LUIGI'S RESTAURANT IN COVENT GARDEN

JOE TAYLOR, HENRY *and* BETTY MCNEIL, FRANKIE LEWIS, PHILIP BROWN *and* KATIE TAYLOR *around a table, towards the end of their meal.*

JOE: (*To* PHILIP) First, that does not mean I am in favour of a nuclear war—

PHILIP: You are arguing for a situation that will make such a war more—

JOE: Let me finish!

(*The rest of the table only half-heartedly listens to this conversation as they finish their meals, sip their coffee, finish their wine, etc.*).

(*To the others*) He twists everything. Anyone else want to jump in, go right ahead. Put me out of my misery.

(*He laughs.*)

PHILIP: (*To the others*) I'm waiting for him to get to Gorbachev—

JOE: Gorbachev supports me! The whole idea of Gorbachev supports my argument! (*To the others*) We got Gorbachev, didn't we? (*Turns to* PHILIP.) Philip, what could be clearer? Please. What I have been

3

saying, the point to be made here is—to go out and protest—. To—. What? Chain yourself to some gate of some plant or some boat or whatever—

PHILIP: Frankie, pass me the last of that wine, please. That's if no one—

HENRY: No, no. It's yours. (*Turns to his wife.*) Betty?

BETTY: I'm fine.

(FRANKIE *passes the wine.* PHILIP *pours into his glass.*)

JOE: If you don't want to—

PHILIP: Go ahead.

(*Beat.*)

JOE: I want to know what's the purpose in all that? In the protesting. What? (*Beat.*) Disarmament??? (*Beat.*) Come on, what does that mean?

FRANKIE: What does dis—?

JOE: When one says one is quote unquote for disarmament, what does one mean? Peace???? (*Beat.*) Who the hell isn't interested in peace?

PHILIP: It's about creating a pressure . . .

JOE: A unilateral pressure? What the hell is that? Is anyone really suggesting—seriously suggesting—that we should just junk our bombs? (*Beat.*) Of course they're not. They are suggesting—demanding that we keep negotiating. Well—I agree! (*Beat.*) If that is the purpose of these adventures, then I agree with them. I agree with the purpose.

PHILIP: But now you'll argue that such actions as these protests, they only make the country weaker which only makes real negotiations less—

JOE: I'm not saying that. Don't paint me into that corner, OK? (*Beat.*) Jesus Christ, I am a goddamn liberal, Philip. (*Beat.*) Listen to me. You are not listening. (*Beat. To the others*) Am I that hard to understand? (*To* PHILIP) If the point of protesting is simply to pressure negotiations. Fine. I understand this. This is not what I'm criticizing. (*Finishes his wine.*) My point is the intellectual dishonesty involved in saying one is for disarmament when everyone is for disarmament. It's like saying you're *for* love!

PHILIP: (*To the others*) There was a time actually not too many years ago—

(*He laughs.*)

JOE: I know. And we learned something from that, didn't we? (*Beat.*) I did. Let's not delude ourselves that we are actually changing things. Or changing much. It is truth, honesty that I'm after. *Say* what you're doing! *Say* what you mean! For Christ's sake is it so hard to be honest? (*Beat.*) I know things are complicated these days, but you know what I think— I think things have always been complicated. (*Beat.*) The man who wrote *Hamlet* understood that the world was complicated.

5

(*Short pause.*)

PHILIP: This is true. Good point.

HENRY: Are we off political science and on to literature now?

PHILIP: If we are, then the perfect example which refutes you, Joe, is that piece of intellectual mush we sat through this afternoon. Talk about idiotic debates.

JOE: (*To the others*) I knew he was getting to this. (*Smiles.*) Look, it's a beautiful play. And that's not just my opinion.

HENRY: It's anthologized—

PHILIP: Straw men—set up to be knocked down. That's how Shaw works. The world presented in that play was *tricky*, not complicated. Shaw enjoyed trickiness, not real thinking.

JOE: And that is one opinion. (*To the others*) Shaw's reputation this half-century has gone up and down, up and down.

(*He laughs.*)

PHILIP: The world today makes such a play ridiculous.

JOE: Come on, it was funny. You laughed.

PHILIP: I laughed. At a play. I didn't appreciate the effort at political argument. Or rather the trivialization of political argument. (*Beat.*) Look, in the end I

6

think we're saying the same thing. The world is complicated. Too complicated for a George Bernard Shaw to express—

JOE: I think that play is very profound.

HENRY: You teach it in your Modern Brit. class, don't you?

JOE: Yes, I do, Henry, thank you. (*Beat. To* PHILIP) It may be a little schematic—

HENRY: You mean a little watered down.

JOE: But a schematic argument sometimes is the best way to present a complex moral position. Breaking the argument apart piece by piece, it illuminates the position. Or the conundrum. If that's what it is. Often in surprising ways. If you'd like I'll show you what I mean.

PHILIP: Look everyone, I'm sorry for getting him started.

FRANKIE: I doubt if you could have stopped him.

JOE: That's not funny.

HENRY: It's interesting, really.

BETTY: Very interesting.

JOE: Thank you. (*To* PHILIP *and* FRANKIE) You want me to show you or not? (*Beat.*) So—capital punishment.

I'll make my point with that. Let me ask Frankie. A woman we all know who has strong moral opinions.

FRANKIE: Since when? (*She laughs.*) He must have got me confused with someone else. How much wine *are* we drinking?

(*Laughter.*)

JOE: Capital punishment, Frankie. Good or bad? (*Beat.*) Come on, good or bad?

FRANKIE: Bad. Of course. Morally indefensible.

JOE: You are sure of that?

FRANKIE: Yes. Yes I am sure, Joe.

JOE: But if I were to present an argument—

FRANKIE: For vengeance? If you believe in vengeance then of course—

JOE: Not vengeance. (*To the others*) Here now is our complicated world at work. (*Beat.*) While I was in grad. school, I was moonlighting for a small paper. I interviewed a guy on death row. A killer. Sentenced to die. Now this was ages ago and his sentence was commuted or whatever—

PHILIP: Before the Supreme Court—

JOE: Yeh. Whatever. Well, Buddy—that's the guy's name; I went to see Buddy. And he started to tell me that *he* favoured the death penalty. A guy on death row!

FRANKIE: Well—a death wish. Like that man in—Where was it? Utah? Nevada?

JOE: No. No, there's no death wish, Frankie. Buddy was pretty sure at this time that his sentence was going to be changed to life. And he was very happy about that. He did not want to die. (*Beat.*) He said that because he was under a death sentence—actually three, he'd murdered three people—the guards in the prison, they knew there was nothing, no recourse left for them if Buddy tried to do something. I mean he was going to die anyway; there was *no* deterrent. Get it? (*Beat.*) So they treated Buddy like an animal. (*Beat.*) Why wouldn't they, right? (*Beat.*) And this—as you can imagine—dehumanized our Buddy. So—he told me—he thought there should be a death penalty for people in prison who had already committed murder but then go ahead and kill a prison guard. This would be his one case when the death penalty would apply.

(*Short pause.*)

PHILIP: Interesting.

JOE: Isn't it?

FRANKIE: I'd never heard—

JOE: Buddy's argument is in favour of treating people like human beings. In this case the threat of death *helps* the prisoner.

HENRY: You should write an article, Joe; you've got something that's publishable.

JOE: Thank you. (*To* FRANKIE) Now you see the problem. As any philosopher knows—you find *one* case that is acceptable, then the *moral* argument falls by the wayside. It's all case by case then, instead of a debate about *morality*.

FRANKIE: Which is what we've achieved with abortion.

JOE: Exactly.

(*Short pause.*)

Don't get me wrong, I think the death penalty is inhuman. I'm just saying, see how tricky things can get? (*Beat.*) Not to wax pretentious, but I do think the mind is really quite extraordinary. (*Beat.*) The pursuit of truth is a bumpy road. But one we all have chosen to follow. Or we wouldn't be teachers.

HENRY: Beautifully said, Joe.

PHILIP: But what the hell does any of that have to do with a hack playwright like Shaw?

(*He laughs; the others laugh.*)

JOE: (*Laughing*) Nothing. Nothing at all, Phil!

(*Pause. They sip their coffee.*)

HENRY: What a provocative discussion.

10

FRANKIE: Katie, this must be very boring for you.

JOE: Nah, she's used to it. She can take it.

KATIE: You should see him at home. Dinner's like a senior seminar.

(*Some light laughter.*)

PHILIP: Lunch with Joe in the canteen is like a senior seminar.

FRANKIE: Mary says being married to him is like living a senior seminar!

(*Laughter.*)

JOE: OK. OK. It's not all that funny. (*Beat. To* KATIE) I hope, young lady, you do not treat all of your teachers with such disrespect.

KATIE: I promise I save all of my disrespect for my father.

(*Laughter.*)

BETTY: Very good!

HENRY: (*Shushing her, under his breath*) Betty!

FRANKIE: (*Over this exchange*) As any child should!

(*Laughter.*)

PHILIP: Or does, you mean!

11

(*Laughter. Pause.* PHILIP *picks up the bill and looks at it.*)

HENRY: Is that the check?

PHILIP: Yes.

(*He hands* HENRY *the bill.*)

BETTY: Katie, your father was telling me this afternoon that you've not been to England before.

KATIE: No. I haven't.

BETTY: How exciting it all must be for you.

KATIE: I'm having a good time. (*Beat.*) The plays are great.

HENRY: Aren't they. (*Puts the bill back down.*) When do we go to Stratford?

JOE: Next Thursday. (*To* FRANKIE) Next Thursday? (*She nods.*)

BETTY: (*To* KATIE) You'll love Stratford.

HENRY: (*To* KATIE) You'll come back to England in maybe ten years, Katie, and it'll all still be here. That's what I love about England. (*Beat.*) We first came ten years ago.

(*Short pause.*)

FRANKIE: Last year's plays were better, I think.

12

BETTY: Do you? Then they must have been really marvellous because so far—

(*She stops herself.*)

FRANKIE: I wasn't saying that this year's—

BETTY: No, no. I know you weren't.

(*Short pause.*)

KATIE: The play today wasn't bad.

JOE: Hear that, Phil? That's one for me. (*To* KATIE) Good for you.

KATIE: The woman who played Barbara, she was great, I thought.

FRANKIE: She *was* good.

HENRY: Excellent.

(*Short pause.*)

KATIE: The Undershaft, wasn't he in *Jewel in the Crown?*

HENRY: Was he?

KATIE: I think so.

PHILIP: Hmmmmmmm. (*To* HENRY) You saw *Jewel in the Crown*, didn't you?

13

HENRY: Not all of it.

PHILIP: Treat yourself. When it comes back on—

BETTY: We will.

(*Short pause.*)

JOE: Mary sends her best.

FRANKIE: You talked to her?

JOE: Katie and I did. (*Beat.*) It's her birthday.

PHILIP: Really? What a shame not to have you—

JOE: She understands. (*Beat.*) It was important to her that Katie could come. So she's happy.

(*Short pause.*)

PHILIP: Well—happy birthday, Mary!

THE OTHERS: Yes, happy birthday.

(*Pause.*)

JOE: Maybe we should pay this. (*Takes the bill. Short pause. Turns to* FRANKIE.) What did you have, Frankie?

FRANKIE: The veal.

JOE: Right. So should I be banker? (*Beat.*) Let's see that's . . .

14

ACT ONE

FRANKIE: (*Takes out money.*) Will this cover it?

JOE: One second.

BETTY: (*To* HENRY) What did we have?

HENRY: I had the lasagne. That was six pounds ten pence.

PHILIP: Plus tax and tip.

FRANKIE: I forgot about the tip.

(*She reaches into her purse for more money.*)

BETTY: (*Putting money down*) This I'm sure will be plenty. (*Beat.*) Won't it?

JOE: And the wine? Do we all put in for the wine?

PHILIP: I certainly do. I must have had—

HENRY: I only had one glass. How much is one glass?

JOE: I'll figure it out. The bottle was—. How many glasses in a bottle?

BETTY: Five. No more than five. They're big glasses.

KATIE: Dad—

JOE: Put your money away, I'll pay for you.

KATIE: But I have money.

15

JOE: Save it. In this town, you'll need it, trust me.

FRANKIE: Did the salad come with the entrée?

KATIE: I had ice-cream.

JOE: I have that.

KATIE: And a coffee.

PHILIP: So did I.

BETTY: Wasn't that an espresso?

PHILIP: Yes, yes, I'm sorry. Is that more?

JOE: One at a time. I have to do one at a time. This is getting too complicated.

SCENE 2

Projection: RYE, EAST SUSSEX

A garden behind a small cottage. A few tables, chairs. A path leads off in one direction. HARRIET BALDWIN, *with a tray of tea, cups, etc., and* KATIE TAYLOR.

HARRIET: They must have gone down the path. He must be showing them Lamb House. If you want to catch up—

KATIE: No, thanks.

16

(Short pause, KATIE rubs her shoulders as HARRIET begins to set a table for tea.)

HARRIET: You're not chilled, are you? We could sit inside. I suppose it may seem a little nippy.

KATIE: I'm fine. I have the sweater. And my coat is just—

HARRIET: *(Not listening)* I find it—. Such weather. I don't know. Just bloody invigorating. One learns after all these years what the British see in their gardens.

(She almost drops a teacup.)

KATIE: Mrs Baldwin, you're sure I can't—

HARRIET: Lamb House is where Henry James lived.

KATIE: I know. Dad read all about it to me on the train.

HARRIET: It's much bigger than this house. He got the gout there.

(Short pause.)

I suppose it's half the reason Professor Baldwin and I have retired here, if the truth be told.

KATIE: So Dad says.

HARRIET: Jamesian Sussex. *(Beat.)* Just the name is quite seductive. Though we very seriously considered Dickensian London. At first I favoured this. We even checked out a flat near the East End. (*Beat.*) The Barbican Towers. Lovely. (*Beat.*) Beautiful fountain. (*Beat.*) Daniel Defoe Tower it was in. We both feel Defoe a very underrated writer. But they gave him a nice tower though. Your father, of course, Katie, kept suggesting Liverpool because of Hawthorne having been consul there. (*Beat.*) We took the train up. (*Beat.*) I don't think your father's ever really been to Liverpool.

KATIE: I don't know.

HARRIET: There's Wordsworth country, of course. We thought of this (*Beat.*) Stratford obviously was out of the question. One might as well be living in Connecticut. (*Beat. Blows on her hands.*) It's not that much warmer in there. The central heating is being put in. If we had known how much that would cost—. But we did get all this for a very modest price. Something like this in the States—. Something historic like this—. (*Beat.*) You couldn't touch it. We couldn't have touched it. (*Beat.*) We consider ourselves very lucky, Katie. Very lucky. (*Finishes setting the table.*) English, isn't it?

KATIE: I'm sorry?

HARRIET: Joe's hooked you for the Department, I understand.

KATIE: Oh. Yes. I'm an English major now.

HARRIET: Excellent. A great Department. Professor Baldwin knew how to pick teachers. So even though

18

we're retired . . . (*Beat.*) You will not be sorry. Our English Department is one of the best Departments in the whole College.

(ORSON BALDWIN, JOE TAYLOR *and* PHILIP BROWN *enter from the path.*)

PHILIP: (*To* ORSON) I stood right up and said—Remember, I was only a sophomore. But I stood there and said to Professor Wilson—. (*To* JOE) Did I ever tell you this?

JOE: I don't know what you're going to say.

PHILIP: About quoting Gandhi to Professor Wilson.

JOE: I don't remember.

PHILIP: I said to him, Orson—something like: Let the judges be judged by the laws they enforce. I don't remember the exact quote. (*Beat.*) But what I meant was: If this faculty disciplinary committee was going to kick me out of school for stopping an army recruiter, then they were going to be judged by the war that recruiter was working for.

JOE: Very nice. Aren't you clever.

ORSON: Who was going to judge them? I don't get it.

PHILIP: I was talking—morally. I was after their consciences.

JOE: Wilson must have been very upset.

19

PHILIP: The most liberal Professor on the campus at the time. Half of my philosophy class with him was on pacifism.

JOE: I took the class. That's why Gandhi's just a brilliant idea.

PHILIP: Let's say I made my point.

JOE: You must have blown his mind.

PHILIP: He hated the war as much as—

ORSON: I'll find the sherry.

(*Beat.*)

JOE: Orson, I'm sorry, we're—

ORSON: Please. Every generation needs its war stories. Sherry, Katie?

JOE: I don't think she's ever even had sherry, have you?

KATIE: I'll pass. But thanks for asking, Professor Baldwin.

(ORSON *leaves in the direction of the house. Short pause.*)

HARRIET: I'm also making tea.

PHILIP: You're spoiling us.

(*Short pause.*)

JOE: Now if I'd tried Gandhi on the town judge . . . (*Beat.*) When *we* stopped our recruiter.

PHILIP: (*To* KATIE) This is a different recruiter. (*To* JOE) He'd either have tarred and feathered you—

JOE: Dumb as a brick, that man. Hated anyone from the College. You know he gave me a suspended sentence. It's still on my record. In some people's eyes even today I'm a criminal, a radical criminal.

HARRIET: In whose eyes? I'm sorry, but I don't understand what you're—

KATIE: They stopped a soldier from recruiting students for the war.

PHILIP: We each did. At different times.

JOE: I had already graduated. But I was still in Middlebury because Mary was still a student. (*Beat.*) Phil was also still a student.

HARRIET: When was this? I haven't heard anything about this.

JOE: Years and years ago, Harriet. The dark ages. (*Beat. To* KATIE *and* PHILIP) Anyway I didn't get any faculty committee, I was arrested. By the police. (*Beat.*) Mary was pregnant with Katie. Fifty dollars for bail. That's what I made in a week at the bookshop.

HARRIET: I'm sorry—which bookshop?

JOE: At the Grange. Before it was a movie theatre.

HARRIET: I loved that bookshop. (*To* KATIE) It had a fireplace.

JOE: It was gas. There wasn't a chimney.

HARRIET: And big chairs. And a cat.

JOE: That was our cat. Before we had Katie, Mary and I had a cat.

PHILIP: I remember that cat. What was its name? Che?

JOE: I don't remember.

KATIE: I think Mom said it was Che.

JOE: Who can remember? (*To* PHILIP) *You* had a dog named Raul.

PHILIP: It wasn't my dog. I didn't feed it.

JOE: You named it.

(*Short pause.*)

PHILIP: How did we get on to . . . ?

JOE: I don't know. (*Beat.*) Orson's Henry James class. And to that from Lamb House.

PHILIP: That's right.

JOE: Philip was saying how he had to cut Orson's class so he could go and stop the recruiter.

PHILIP: I didn't ask. I just did it. I was a sophomore.

HARRIET: You had to have been a good student to get into his James seminar as a sophomore.

PHILIP: This was second semester.

HARRIET: Still.

KATIE: And Professor Baldwin, he was understanding . . . about your cutting the class.

(ORSON *enters with the sherry and glasses.*)

PHILIP: No, he tried to flunk me. He didn't even stop there, he tried to get me kicked out of school. I thought he was a fascist. To this day, I can't help tying Henry James to fascism.

(*He laughs.*)

JOE: Not completely off the mark.

HARRIET: (*To* ORSON) Dear, I think these young men are calling you a fascist.

(ORSON *shrugs and sets down the drinks.*)

JOE: Orson, you really tried to kick Philip out of school?

ORSON: I tried to kick them all out. (*Beat.*) As for you, I might have even talked to the town judge. I thought you should get at least six months. In a prison.

(*Short pause.*)

23

You weren't a student any more so of course I was speaking only as a concerned citizen. (*Beat.*) I think I talked to him. I wanted to at least.

(*Pause.*)

JOE: (*Suddenly laughs.*) You're joking.

ORSON: No.

(*Pause.*)

PHILIP: (*To* JOE) He tried to get you thrown into—?

JOE: But you hired me—both of us—right out of grad. school. You brought us into the Department.

ORSON: In life, you take one thing at a time. (*Downs his sherry.*) My understanding was that my students were in college to study. Those who wished not to or had better, more relevant things to do, were welcome to go do them.

(*Pause.*)

PHILIP: (*Changing the subject*) Lamb House is quite beautiful, Katie. If you feel like it you really should go and take a look. (*To* ORSON) James spent what? Maybe twenty years there.

ORSON: Didn't you read the plaque?

(FRANKIE LEWIS *comes out of the house; as she does she puts on her coat.*)

24

FRANKIE: No one's been murdered by terrorists today. Though Donna Silliman has left her passport on a bus.

ORSON: Silliman? Is that Jewish?

JOE: No.

(*Beat. Confused,* JOE *looks at the others.*)

I think her background's Greek. But what does that have to do with anything?

(ORSON *shrugs.*)

FRANKIE: Henry's taking her to the Embassy.

ORSON: Henry?

PHILIP: Henry McNeil. He and his wife are with us as well.

ORSON: Really? The Department is that affluent now?

(*He laughs to himself and shakes his head. Short pause.*)

PHILIP: (*To* FRANKIE) If you feel like it, Lamb House is just—

HARRIET: No one ever lost their passport when we ran the trip. (*Beat.*) What sort of girl is this one?

ORSON: She's not Jewish.

25

HARRIET: I heard this, Orson.

(*Beat.*)

JOE: Well—. She's—. (*Beat.*) She's smart. (*Beat.*) She's fine. Isn't she, Katie? Katie knows her.

KATIE: I don't *know* her. I've talked to her a few times. She's OK. She's really OK. (*Beat.*) I like her.

(*Short pause.*)

JOE: (*To* ORSON) Katie likes her.

(ORSON *nods and pours himself another sherry.* JOE *looks to* FRANKIE *and to* PHILIP.)

Orson, since Henry McNeil's name has come up on its own. Would you have a minute or two for business?

(*Short pause.*)

ORSON: (*Nodding towards* KATIE) What about . . . ?

JOE: Katie, maybe you should go take a look at Lamb House now.

HARRIET: Or come inside with me. I was just about to make the salad.

KATIE: I'd be happy to help, Mrs Baldwin. (*To the others, as they go*) I understand. Department business.

(*They go into the house.*)

JOE: It was easier, Orson, when she wasn't going to the College. She wasn't interested in anything we talked about then. Anyway, about Henry.

ORSON: I know what you—

JOE: You probably do, but let me say it anyway.

ORSON: And I told you—

JOE: I know you did, but please, Orson, I'm the Chairman of the Department now, not you.

(Short pause.)

Sorry.

ORSON: Never be sorry for saying the truth.

(Short pause.)

JOE: The Dean says—. (*To* PHILIP *and* FRANKIE) Correct me if I misstate. (*To* ORSON) He says that we either release Henry after this term or offer him tenure track. It's no more one-year contracts. (*Beat.*) Of course he's right. It isn't fair to anyone.

ORSON: No. It isn't. (*Beat.*) But I gather, Mr Chairman, that you don't wish to offer him—

JOE: His degree, Orson, it's from Case Western Reserve. That's not exactly Harvard.

ORSON: No.

27

JOE: That is not our standard.

ORSON: No.

PHILIP: He's been great to have though. Really filled the gaps. Who else was going to teach Milton?

FRANKIE: He's a dear, lovely man.

PHILIP: And Betty—. Everyone adores her.

JOE: They paid their own way here. He wanted that much to come. (*Beat.*) I guess he felt if he came then—

ORSON: He's here to kiss ass, is that what you want to say?

JOE: No. I'm not—. I wouldn't put it that way. (*Beat.*) He's not official. His being here. That's all I meant to say.

(*Pause.*)

PHILIP: (*Finally*) Any advice, Orson?

ORSON: (*Turns to them*) If you're talking about next year—

JOE: We are.

ORSON: Then you'd better start interviewing, it's already—

JOE: We have.

28

(*Beat.*)

ORSON: Then McNeil already knows.

JOE: No. (*Beat.*) No, he doesn't.

PHILIP: He's hoping for one more year. He's been applying all over the place. But he's set his sights a little too high, we think.

ORSON: Of course! We've spoiled him!

FRANKIE: He's had a couple of close calls.

JOE: Henry getting something, that would be the answer. That's the hope.

ORSON: Yes, that would let you off the hook.

(*He laughs to himself. Short pause.*)

I don't see what choice you have but to tell him. Especially as you've begun to interview.

JOE: We've offered someone his job actually.

ORSON: Then—

JOE: (*Turns to* PHILIP *and* FRANKIE.) Young woman out of Yale. Very bright, isn't she? She'll teach Milton as well. Seems to be he's even a hobby of hers, if you can believe that.

(*He laughs. No one else does.*)

(*To* ORSON) She hasn't *signed* the contract. I guess we could lose her. I had thought that maybe we shouldn't tell Henry until we were absolutely sure we had this new person. I didn't want to get the Department in a hole.

ORSON: No. You don't want to do that. Never do that. (*Beat.*) The problem then is—what to tell Henry now.

JOE: I know you've had to deal with things like this before.

PHILIP: He's spent a lot of money, just the airfares for him and Betty—

ORSON: Have you thought about telling McNeil the truth?

(JOE *looks to* FRANKIE *and* PHILIP.)

JOE: We've been telling him the truth, Orson. You don't think that we've been lying—?

ORSON: I mean all the truth. Everything. Tell him he's out. Come next year that is the fact, isn't it?

JOE: Yes, but—.

(JOE *looks to* PHILIP *and* FRANKIE.)

Yes. That is the fact. Even if this woman from Yale doesn't—. I have a file of at least ten others.

ORSON: I'm thinking of the Department now. (*Turns and points his finger at* JOE.) As you should be, Joe.

30

(*Beat.*) The longer you wait the more resentful he's going to be. This sort of situation, it can cause a lot of shit. Suddenly you have a teacher who isn't bothering to teach any more. This has happened, Joe.

JOE: I know the case you're talking about.

PHILIP: If that's the thinking, why not just tell Henry the last day of classes when he can't do any harm? (*Beat.*) I'm not suggesting this.

ORSON: It wouldn't work. He'd have forced the issue weeks before with the Dean. (*Beat.*) You tell him now, you also tell him he's got a recommendation from you whenever he needs it. Whether he's resentful or not *there's* his reason for behaving himself.

(*Pause.*)

JOE: Then the right thing seems to be to tell him. (*Beat.*) The truth.

ORSON: If I were you.

(*Short pause.*)

PHILIP: I agree with Orson. We should tell him.

FRANKIE: We have to, Joe. (*Beat. To* PHILIP) I love Henry, don't you?

(*Short pause.*)

JOE: Then—OK. (*To* FRANKIE *and* PHILIP) I'll do it. While we're here, I'll do it. (*Beat.*) This week I'll—

(*Beat.*) Tomorrow I will do it. (*Beat.*) Thanks, Orson. Thanks for your wisdom.

(ORSON *nods and pours himself more sherry.*)

ORSON: (*As he pours*) Too bad Henry's not black. He'd get a job like that. (*Snaps his fingers.*)

PHILIP: Orson, that's—

(*He stops himself.*)

ORSON: How are the children, Frankie?

FRANKIE: Great. (*Beat.*) And Howard's great too. Sends his best.

JOE: Howard was given the Stirling Biology Chair, you know.

ORSON: I read this in the *Alumni Review.* Congratulations.

(HARRIET *and* KATIE *come out.*)

HARRIET: Can we come out now? You looked from the window like you were winding down.

ORSON: I'm sorry, we didn't mean to—

HARRIET: Dinner will be ready in ten minutes.

(*They sit. Pause.*)

ORSON: Anyone want more sherry?

(They shake their heads.)

HARRIET: So how many students do you have with you this year?

JOE: It's twenty-two, isn't it? Counting Katie.

KATIE: Why wouldn't you count me, I'm a student.

JOE: And we've seen what? Fifteen plays so far, in the first two and a half weeks. Another, I think—

PHILIP: Twelve or thirteen to go.

FRANKIE: We've seen some wonderful things. We'll be in Stratford later this week.

ORSON: The students will love that. When I ran this course Stratford was always the highpoint.

(Short pause. He laughs to himself.)

I remember a *Much Ado* we saw—

JOE: I think I was with you that year.

FRANKIE: We saw a *Misanthrope* that was very funny, Orson.

ORSON: I don't like French plays. I don't know why.

PHILIP: There was the Shaw. Katie just loved the Shaw.

KATIE: *(Smiling)* I didn't say I loved it that much!

33

JOE: Don't back down now!

(*He laughs. All except the* BALDWINS *laugh.*)

ORSON: Shaw is very underestimated today. Very. You know they've discovered some letters between James and Shaw. Very interesting.

HARRIET: You've been to the National, I suppose.

FRANKIE: A few times already. It's like nothing else, is it?

(*Short pause.*)

PHILIP: At one of the buffets we had a main course and wine and it cost what?

FRANKIE: Five pounds at the most.

JOE: Not even that much.

PHILIP: It was under three. I mean, it was cheap.

SCENE 3

Projection: FOYLE'S BOOKSHOP, STREET LEVEL

A large table full of books with only their spines showing (*the sale table*). JOE TAYLOR, PHILIP BROWN *and* HENRY MCNEIL *browse through the books on the table. Pause.* PHILIP *picks out a book.*

PHILIP: (*To* JOE) Have you read this?

JOE: Oh God.

PHILIP: I know what you mean.

(*He puts the book back. Pause.*)

HENRY: (*With a book*) This I found pretty interesting.

JOE: Did you?

(*Pause. They browse.*)

PHILIP: (*With another book*) I think he really missed the boat on Whitman.

JOE: He's good on Irving though.

PHILIP: I didn't realize anyone even read him on Irving any more. (*Beat.*) I didn't realize anyone read Irving any more.

(PHILIP *looks to* HENRY.)

HENRY: I don't.

(JOE *picks up a book.*)

PHILIP: What's that?

JOE: (*Putting it back*) Second printing. (*Picks up another.*) Ever met him?

PHILIP: Booth? No.

JOE: You should, it's an experience.

35

HENRY: I question some of the things he has had to say about Conrad.

PHILIP: You do?

(*Beat.*)

HENRY: You know I did my thesis on Conrad.

PHILIP: Then you should know.

(*Short pause.*)

(*Looking at the picture of Booth on the book*) We shared a table at the MLA one day. If you'd had to watch him eat, you'd never read a word he wrote again.

(PHILIP *has taken the book and now puts it back.*)

At least not on art.

JOE: (*Without looking up*) In Chicago? (*Beat.*) Was the MLA that year in Chicago?

PHILIP: (*Browsing*) Atlanta.

(*Beat.*)

HENRY: I was at the one in Chicago.

(*Pause.*)

JOE: Philip was there too, weren't you? You brought that native American Indian woman to dinner with us. To this day, Mary thinks he's interested in native American literature.

PHILIP: I've done some research! (*Then laughs.*) She was beautiful. Made Chicago almost bearable. Though I do remember being tired all the time.

(*He laughs.*)

JOE: (*To* HENRY) And Mary keeps saying he needs to be fixed up. That's how little she understands men.

(*They browse.*)

Jesus Christ. (*Picks up a book.*) This is the sort of thing that should be burned. (*Opens it.*) I know for a fact that he spent just two years on Hawthorne at the Princeton Library. In and out of Hawthorne scholarship in two years! And he writes a book. (*Beat.*) Junk. Nothing's digested. This is the sort of thing that drives me crazy. (*Beat. He puts book back, continues to browse.*)

(*Without looking up*) I reviewed it for the *Hawthorne Quarterly*. You'd think I'd raped his daughter, the letter he wrote me.

(*He laughs.*)

PHILIP: I don't see anything I want here. I'm going upstairs to drama.

JOE: I'll stay down here with Henry.

HENRY: I was thinking of going—

JOE: Stay with me. Come on.

(HENRY *looks to* PHILIP.)

I'd like the company.

(*Beat.*)

PHILIP: We'll meet here in an hour and then go to Dillons.

JOE: Fine.

PHILIP: (*To* HENRY) OK?

HENRY: Sure. Yeh. I didn't know we were—

PHILIP: Where's Betty?

HENRY: She's probably in fiction.

PHILIP: Good for her. That's where I'd be if I only had the time. (*As he leaves.*) She can come to Dillons as well of course.

(*He goes. Short pause.*)

JOE: I thought that went without saying. About Betty coming with us.

HENRY: It does. Of course it does.

JOE: Show me what you're getting?

HENRY: (*Picks up the pile of paperbacks at his feet.*) I'll probably put a few back.

JOE: Huh. (*Beat.*) Nice. The Penguins though you probably can get half off. There are a million places that—. Just down the street, at the Penguin Shop, in the basement. They're used, but . . .

HENRY: I wouldn't care about that. I happen to even prefer used paperbacks. It's sort of a thing of mine . . .

JOE: I'd look there first.

HENRY: Thanks. I'll put these back.

JOE: Henry? (*Beat.*) Also, on the corner—

HENRY: The used shop. I've been—

JOE: With the green front.

HENRY: Right. I know, when you go in—

JOE: Also in the cellar. There's a whole room of Penguins.

HENRY: There are? (*Beat.*) Terrific.

(*Long pause.* JOE *slowly checks out* HENRY's *pile of books.* HENRY *pretends to browse.*)

JOE: Just wanted to save you some money.

HENRY: I appreciate it. I do. (*Beat.*) So I guess now I can buy a few more books. (*Laughs.*) It's a disease, it really is, isn't it? That's what Betty calls it. She says that if I were given the choice between a last meal or a last book, I'd—

JOE: (*Not listening; looking through one of his books*) I hadn't realized . . .

HENRY: What? (*Beat.*) Looks interesting, doesn't it? I figure if I'm teaching Milton I might as well—. You know.

JOE: That's quite admirable.

(*Pause.*)

HENRY: I love teaching Milton actually.

JOE: That's—lucky.

(JOE *laughs, then* HENRY *joins in, a little nervously. Short pause.*)

(*Going back to browsing*) No luck with the job hunt, I suppose.

HENRY: You'd be the first to hear, Joe. After Betty. Of course.

JOE: Right, I didn't think—. (*Stops himself.*) She's incredibly well liked, you know. One hears that all the time.

(HENRY *nods.*)

HENRY: Joe. I know it'd make life a lot easier for you, if I got—

JOE: That is so like you, Henry! (*Beat.*) Here you are, with a problem, and what do you do? You worry about me? (*Pats him on the back.*) You are something.

HENRY: It's a tight market out there.

JOE: Tell me about it. The number of applications I get . . . You wouldn't want to know. (*Beat.*) But I've got to think, you—. Henry, you!

(*Pause.* JOE *pretends to browse again.*)

HENRY: Joe, if I ask you something, you'll be honest with me, won't you?

JOE: You have to ask that??

HENRY: I mean it. The truth, OK? (*Beat.*) Not just for me, but for Betty and the kids. I just need to know.

JOE: Henry, what are you talking about?

HENRY: I know maybe I should have waited for you to bring it up. But it's why you wanted to talk to me, isn't it? Why you didn't want me to go with—?

JOE: Henry, you're not making any sense.

(*Pause.*)

HENRY: Joe, is there *any* chance of my keeping my job past June? (*Beat.*) Look, I've accepted that tenure

41

track is out of the question. I've put that out of my mind.

JOE: That—was a good thing to do. (*Beat.*) I would not count on getting tenure track.

HENRY: No. (*Laughs to himself.*) I don't any more. But still with one more year under my belt. One more year and, Joe, I'd be pretty damn attractive to a lot of colleges.

JOE: You're attractive to a lot of colleges already, Henry. You just need to get a little lucky.

HENRY: I do have two interviews lined up.

JOE: (*Big smile*) Now that's good to hear! Great for you, Henry. I told everyone it would only be a matter of time.

HENRY: They're both with high schools, Joe.

(*Short pause.*)

JOE: Oh shit.

HENRY: Is there *any* chance at all of my staying on for one more year? I'm not asking for a definite yes, just is there a chance? (*Beat.*) You know I'd teach anything.

JOE: That's never been an issue.

HENRY: If I had a whole year more. You see what I'm saying. There's hardly anything out there now.

Whereas next year, I know for sure of three positions, because of retirements . . .

(JOE *is looking back at the table of books.*)

I'm sorry, if this isn't the right time. You want to look at—

JOE: (*Looks up.*) No. No.

(*Short pause.*)

HENRY: Have you already hired someone to replace me? (*Beat.*) You have, haven't you?

JOE: Who told you that? Henry, with you still thinking that you could be hired back?

HENRY: Then you haven't?

JOE: We've interviewed. Of course.

HENRY: I've heard this. This does not surprise me. That's OK.

JOE: I wouldn't want to give you a lot of hope.

HENRY: I'm not asking for a lot. (*Short pause.*) Joe. Look at me and tell me.

JOE: (*Looks at him.*) No one's been hired yet. No.

HENRY: OK. Good. (*Breathes deeply.*) Excellent. Thank you. Just to have this talk has made this trip worthwhile. I'll go find Betty and tell her we're going to Dillons.

JOE: And put those Penguins back and save yourself some money.

HENRY: I will. I'll do that. Thanks. Thanks a lot, Joe.

(*He turns to go, sees* BETTY *who has just entered.*)

There you are.

BETTY: The system they have in this store, it drives me crazy. First you have to find the book. Then you stand in one line to get a bill, you take the bill to the cash line, you pay the cash person, then you go back—

HENRY: Buy it at Dillons. We're going there next.

BETTY: Are we?

JOE: Actually I'm set to go any time. We just have to find Philip.

HENRY: I'll find him. I have to put these books back anyway.

JOE: He's up in drama.

HENRY: That's what he said.

(*He turns to go, then back to* BETTY.)

You don't mind? About Dillons?

BETTY: No.

HENRY: Good. Thanks.

(*He hurries off.* JOE *goes back to looking through the books. Pause.*)

BETTY: You didn't tell him, did you, Joe?

(JOE *looks up.*)

JOE: About?

BETTY: You've hired his replacement. (*Beat.*) Frankie told me last night after all of you got back from the Baldwins'.

JOE: She did, did she.

BETTY: I asked her and she told me. I knew you'd have been talking about Henry's situation. And Frankie had the guts to tell me the truth.

JOE: Betty, how do you know what I've told Henry and what I haven't told—

BETTY: He won't even go to his interviews, Joe! He's dreaming. And what are we supposed to do? I don't even know where we'll live. Do you know how much this trip cost? Do you know why he insisted we come? (*Beat.*) He was hoping if we hung around with—

JOE: I know!!!

(*Short pause.*)

45

It is going to break his heart to teach high school.

BETTY: True enough.

JOE: (*Turns on her.*) You want to break his heart?!!!

BETTY: That doesn't make sense, Joe.

(*Pause.*)

JOE: I only want to be kind. I think there is a place for kindness in this world! A place for caring! For decency!

(*Short pause. He rubs his eyes, then leans on the table, sighs.*)

Look. I talked to him, OK? Two minutes ago.

BETTY: You told him? You actually told him you'd hired—?

JOE: You saw how he looked. You can thank me for being so gentle with him.

BETTY: And he understood you? (*Beat.*) And he understood you?!

JOE: I was as clear as I could be, Betty. I can't do any more than that.

BETTY: I suppose not.

(*Short pause.*)

46

JOE: You know Henry. He dreams. He hears what he wants to hear sometimes.

BETTY: OK.

JOE: But if you're saying what I should have done was shove the fact in his face, well—

BETTY: No, Joe, no.

JOE: I did the best I could. And it was one of the hardest things I've ever had to do to a friend. And Henry is my friend, Betty.

(*Beat. She nods.*)

So it is done. It's done. Now enough is enough.

(*He starts to browse again.*)

I even saved him some money on some books.

BETTY: Thank you.

JOE: (*Picks up a book.*) Catch!

(*He throws her the book. She catches it.*)

I understand you like fiction. I hear that's good. I don't have much time for fiction myself . . . (*Beat.*) Let me buy that for you. I think it's only 50p.

SCENE 4

Projection: LYTTELTON BUFFET

JOE TAYLOR *and* JOANNE SMITH *sit at a table; pastry and tea in front of them;* JOANNE *has a small shoebox beside her.*

JOANNE: No, I didn't mean that! I love Stratford. I really do. And the Royal Shakespeare Company, it's—. It's world famous, isn't it? What more could you want? (*Beat.*) It's just—

JOE: Joanne, I know what you're going to say.

JOANNE: I don't think you can—

JOE: You're going to say, the problem with Stratford is—. Well, to be brutally blunt, it's all the Americans. Right?

JOANNE: How did you—?

JOE: Look, I feel the same way. Every time I go there it drives me crazy.

JOANNE: You too? Professor Taylor, I can't tell you how—

JOE: I don't know what it is about the place. Attracts them like flies.

JOANNE: London's not nearly so bad.

JOE: They at least hesitate in London.

48

JOANNE: By and large they do.

JOE: But in Stratford! Last year I think six different people came up to me. I hadn't said anything. I had even avoided eye contact. But if they sniff you out as an American—

JOANNE: Which in Stratford does not take a blood-hound.

JOE: I tried once wearing a nice tweed cap. I loved this cap. Some guy from Louisiana nearly knocks me down, he was so excited to tell me he'd brought the same sort of cap in Edinburgh.*

JOANNE: I know they come right at you.

JOE: Why do I care where they're from, this is what I don't understand. So they happen to be American and so am I. So big deal.

JOANNE: Right.

JOE: We have nothing in common. I don't know—. They make the whole thing feel cheap.

JOANNE: By 'the whole thing' you mean being here.

JOE: Absolutely.

JOANNE: I get that same feeling.

JOE: For you it must be—. Because you're actually liv-

* JOE *pronounces the* gh *as a strong* g.

49

ing here. You're a resident and everything. (*Beat.*) Then to be taken for a tourist.

JOANNE: It drives me crazy. So I hardly go to Stratford any more. And never. Never in the summer.

JOE: *That* must be a nightmare. The summer.

JOANNE: Imagine your worst nightmare and then double it.

(*Pause. They sip their tea.*)

JOE: (*Takes a bite of a pastry.*) Delicious. Would you like to try—?

(*She shakes her head.*)

JOANNE: I used to feel a little funny about it. They are after all from my country. But—. (*Beat.*) Then you hear them shout.

JOE: (*Eating*) If they just acted like they were guests.

JOANNE: My husband doesn't mind. He finds them sort of—

JOE: But he's not American. So he's not the one being embarrassed.

JOANNE: That's true. Well put. (*Beat.*) I'll explain it that way to him.

(*Short pause.*)

50

Sometimes when I'm in a shop I try not to say anything. I just point. Maybe they'll think I'm English or something. Maybe that I don't even speak English. That I'm foreign. So I point.

JOE: The accents some people have.

JOANNE: They don't hear themselves. (*Beat.*) Sometimes it's funny, but sometimes—

(*Short pause.*)

Anyway.

JOE: Right. Anyway.

(*She starts to open the box.*)

JOANNE: It's good to talk to someone who—. Well—. You know.

JOE: I know. (*Offering her the last bite of pastry*) Are you sure?

JOANNE: No, thanks.

(*She starts to take out piles of tickets with rubber bands around them.*)

JOE: (*Eating the last bite*) Incredible, the calibre of food sold in a theatre.

JOANNE: Here's the last lot.

JOE: (*Eating*) Everyone—by the way—has been raving about the seats we've had.

JOANNE: Good, I'm pleased to hear that. You never really know what you'll get.

JOE: I don't think we've had one bad seat.

JOANNE: Knock wood. So—here's for this afternoon, the Lyttelton. It's wonderful by the way. You'll have a great time.

JOE: Terrific.

JOANNE: (*Handing over bunches of tickets*) The Simon Gray is tonight. (*Beat.*) It's short. (*Beat.*) Tomorrow's Stratford. Thursday's Stratford again. Friday's the day off. That's correct, isn't it?

JOE: (*Going over his list that he has taken out*) That's correct.

JOANNE: Good. (*Beat.*) Then there's Saturday back at the Barbican. Monday, the Royal Court.

JOE: What's there?

JOANNE: I forget. It's in previews.

JOE: Oh really. That could be fun.

JOANNE: Something very Royal Courtish to be sure.

JOE: I know what you mean.

(*He laughs to himself.*)

JOANNE: I finally got *Les Mis.* on Tuesday.

JOE: Thank you. Mary and I saw it in New York. The kids'll love it.

JOANNE: Something at Wyndham's on Wednesday afternoon, then a free evening and you're gone on Thursday. So there you have the rest of it. (*Pushing the box of tickets toward him*) James, I'm afraid, is working late these days in the City. He sends his regrets about Wednesday night.

JOE: (*Looking at the tickets*) I'm sorry to hear—

JOANNE: But if you wouldn't mind my coming alone . . .

JOE: (*Looks up.*) Alone? Of course not! Why would we mind? (*Beat.*) James must be doing very well.

JOANNE: He is. He is. (*Beat.*) We're going to buy a boat.

(*Beat.*)

JOE: We haven't decided on the restaurant. But I'll—

JOANNE: There's no rush. I'm home most nights. (*Beat.*) And there's a machine.

JOE: I'll call. When we've decided.

JOANNE: Good.

(PHILIP BROWN *has entered with a tray.*)

PHILIP: Joe, would you excuse me for a second? (*To* JOANNE) Sorry to interrupt.

JOE: Philip, you haven't met Joanne Smith.

PHILIP: I don't believe I—

JOE: Joanne, Philip Brown.

JOANNE: How do you do?

PHILIP: How do you do? (*To* JOE) I don't mean to—

JOE: Joanne's the one who bought us the theatre tickets.

PHILIP: Oh right! Joe's former student. Wonderful seats. Every show's been great.

JOE: (*To* JOANNE) See what I mean? (*To* PHILIP) Come and sit with us.

PHILIP: Frankie's in line—

JOE: She can join us too. Sit down. Come on, there's room.

(PHILIP *puts his tray down.*)

And now—tell us what's the news on the Rialto?

(*He laughs. No one else does.*)

54

PHILIP: Donna Silliman's still missing.

JOE: (*Looks at his watch.*) She's going to miss another play. What do some of these kids think they're here for?!

JOANNE: What's this—?

PHILIP: One of our students, she wasn't in her room last night, and—. Well, you heard.

JOE: I just do not understand this kind of thing!

JOANNE: But I guess it's got to happen all the time.

PHILIP: Every year. Something happens every year.

JOE: This one's already lost her passport once.

JOANNE: There's always one.

PHILIP: We got from one of the students that she's been seeing some boy. From Amherst, if you can believe it. He's with another school group. We're trying to find out what hotel they're staying in.

JOE: You've called Amherst?

PHILIP: Frankie did. She charged it to your room. It didn't seem fair to have it on her expenses.

JOE: That's fair.

PHILIP: It seems that yesterday and today—Frankie should tell you herself—but these are their free days

55

and the students have been encouraged to travel around a little bit. So Donna probably went with the guy somewhere.

JOE: So she'll be back tomorrow. When we're in Stratford. (*Beat.*) Great.

PHILIP: She probably hasn't thought to look at the schedule.

JOANNE: I am sure it will all work out.

JOE: (*To* PHILIP) Speaking of Frankie, where was she last night?

PHILIP: Last night? We were all at the theatre. What was the name of that play? After a while they begin to blurr, don't they?

JOANNE: I can check the—.

(*She takes out her schedule.*)

JOE: I mean later. After Katie told me about Donna, I knocked on Frankie's door.

PHILIP: And she didn't answer?

(JOE *shakes his head.*)

That's funny. (*Shrugs.*) I don't know. Maybe she's a sound sleeper, Joe. (*Beat.*) Why are you asking me?

JOANNE: It was *Les Liaisons Dangereuses.*

PHILIP: What was?

JOANNE: The play you saw last night.

PHILIP: That's right. With the girl with the naked back. I remember that one.

(FRANKIE LEWIS *enters with a tray.*)

FRANKIE: Is there room for—

JOE: Of course there is. Philip, move over.

FRANKIE: I could sit—

JOE: No. No. (*To* JOANNE) Frankie Lewis, Joanne Smith.

PHILIP: Joanne's the woman who—

FRANKIE: Yes, we met the other day. Katie introduced us.

JOANNE: Yes, that's right.

FRANKIE: Each day the seats get even better. (*Nods to* PHILIP.) Philip.

PHILIP: Frankie.

FRANKIE: Phil's told you, I gather.

PHILIP: Told what?

JOE: That we have a runaway.

57

PHILIP: That. Yes, he knows.

FRANKIE: I wouldn't say 'runaway'. That's a little melodramatic, wouldn't you say? She'll be back.

JOE: When we're in Stratford.

FRANKIE: They're not children, Joe. (*To* JOANNE) You were a student of Joe's.

JOE: My first year teaching.

JOANNE: I even babysat for Katie. (*To* JOE) I didn't tell you, we had tea one afternoon last week. She's really—. She's grown up.

FRANKIE: (*To* JOE) That's where we ran into each other. At the Tate.

JOANNE: Right. And Katie introduced us.

FRANKIE: (*Picking up the Hamleys bag that she brought with her*) This is in your way.

JOANNE: No, it's—

FRANKIE: I'll set it over here. (*She does.*) Something for the boys from Hamleys.

JOE: Frankie has two beautiful boys.

JOANNE: Congratulations.

(*Short pause. Suddenly* PHILIP *laughs to himself.*)

PHILIP: It's funny—but when I first came in and saw Joe talking with a strange attractive young woman—

JOE: Joanne Smith.

PHILIP: I know. But I didn't know then. I didn't know you knew her, Joe. (*Shakes his head and laughs.*) So my first thought, seeing these two, was—now that is so unlike Joe Taylor. (*Laughs.*) But then it turns out you do know her. She even used to babysit . . .

(*He laughs. Others are confused about what he is saying.*)

Never mind.

(*Pause.*)

FRANKIE: (*To* JOE) Donna Silliman will come back to the hotel, find we're gone, we'll leave a message and she can take a train and join us or wait for us. (*Beat.*) What else can we do?

PHILIP: Oh Joe, you wanted to ask Frankie about last night?

FRANKIE: (*Turns to* PHILIP) What about last night?

JOE: I knocked—

PHILIP: He knocked on your door. What time was that?

JOE: About—four.

PHILIP: About four, he knocked. *I* told him you must be a very sound sleeper.

FRANKIE: Well I am, Joe. (*Beat.*) I am a very sound sleeper. Everyone knows that.

PHILIP: Hopefully, not everyone.

(*He laughs. Then the others laugh. Finally* FRANKIE *joins in.*)

FRANKIE: I don't know about anyone else, but I'm still getting over my jet lag. (*Beat.*) But at least I don't go dozing off in the middle of a show.

JOE: Once! The second night we're here!

FRANKIE: (*To* JOANNE) He refused to take a nap.

PHILIP: He kept saying he'd taken this trip so many times, he didn't need a—

JOE: OK! OK! (*Beat.*) Christ, will you ever let me forget it?

(*Short pause.*)

FRANKIE: I'm sorry I didn't hear you knock.

(JOE *nods. Beat.*)

JOE: Joanne's been to the play we're seeing this afternoon. She loved it.

60

JOANNE: It's very funny. I love those old Aldwych farces. They're so English.

JOE: They really are.

JOANNE: I don't think they'd work at all in America today, do you?

JOE: I can't see how. It takes a special . . .

JOANNE: I know what you mean. (*Beat.*) James's family is right out of one of those plays actually. (*Laughs to herself.*) The first time I met them—. They don't live posh or anything like that, but there is a cook. She used to be James's nanny. (*Beat.*) One of the family, she is. And everyone is always saying that. Helen from Glasgow. (*Beat.*) They could not have been kinder to me. James's father, Freddy—he insists I call him Freddy—and once he gets into a chair you begin to wonder if he'll ever move out of it. (*Beat.*) Or so his mother says. James's sister made us all watch the telly. James tried to argue but I said I'd love to. I'd only been here a month and I'd hardly got used to English telly so I thought here was my chance to ask questions. (*Beat.*) So this man comes on; he tries to make some jokes which are not funny, I think to myself. Then he says something like: 'The girl went up to the boy and put her hand into his—.' He paused and a middle-aged woman completes the sentence with: '—her hand into his *golf bag!*' And everyone laughs. (*Beat.*) Even James laughed I noticed. This is peculiar I think to myself. (*Beat.*) 'Into his golf bag.' She continues now '—and pulls out a club which she used to wiggle his—.' She pauses and a middle-aged

61

man now completes the sentence with: 'Wiggle his *tee* out of the ground.'

(*Short pause. She sips her tea.*)

JOE: Huh.

JOANNE: This goes on and on. And when it ends the man who started it all drops his trousers to reveal that his underpants look like the British flag.

(*Short pause.*)

What's amazing about England is that in time you begin to find this sort of thing funny as well. (*Beat.*) Or so I'm told. James says it's the weather. (*Beat.*) In any event, I don't think a good old Aldwych farce would work in America.

JOE: No.

PHILIP: No.

(*Pause.*)

FRANKIE: Have you lived in London long, Joanne?

JOANNE: About sixteen and a half months.

(*Short pause.*)

PHILIP: It must have been a lot of work getting us the tickets.

JOANNE: It was fun. I love it. (*Beat.*) I love going to the theatre. Even going to the box office. It's something to do. (*Beat.*) Professor Taylor, I'd love to do it again next year.

JOE: (*Hardly before she's finished*) Consider yourself hired! (*To the others*) Right?

FRANKIE: Absolutely.

PHILIP: You're the Chairman!

JOANNE: Thanks. Thank you. (*Beat. Beginning to stand up*) I should be going. You all probably have a million things to do.

JOE: Us? No. We have nothing to do. What time's the show?

FRANKIE: Two thirty.

JOE: Two thirty. We've got another hour.

(JOANNE *sits back down. Pause.*)

(*Finally*) Frankie, I'm sure I don't need to say this, but I do think we should try to keep it to ourselves.

FRANKIE: Keep what to ourselves??

JOE: That Katie was the one who told us about Donna Silliman not being in her room. (*Beat.*) Last night. Before I knocked on your door. And you were asleep. (*Beat.*) I don't want the kids to start thinking she's a . . .

63

PHILIP: Spy?

JOE: Yeh. I guess. Yeh.

JOANNE: That must be hard for Katie.

JOE: She handles it well.

JOANNE: Oh, I'm sure she—

JOE: There's Henry and Betty.

(HENRY *and* BETTY MCNEIL *enter with trays.*)

Over here! There's room over here! (*To the others*)
Let's squish together a little more.

(*They do.*)

BETTY: You're too crowded. We'll sit outside.

JOE: It's raining.

BETTY: It stopped.

JOE: It's wet then.

HENRY: If you think there's room.

JOE: Of course there's room.

(*Everyone starts to squeeze together;* JOANNE *stands.*)

JOANNE: Actually, look at the time. I should be off.

HENRY: I hope that we're not—

JOE: There's plenty of—

JOANNE: Really. I just noticed the time. Thanks.

(*She goes. They sit.*)

PHILIP: She's the one who bought the tickets.

HENRY: Oh. (*Stands and shouts*) Beautiful seats!!!

JOE: Don't shout.

HENRY: What?

JOE: Never mind.

(*Long pause.*)

(*To* PHILIP) What if she gets pregnant?

(PHILIP *quickly turns to* FRANKIE *then back to* JOE.)

PHILIP: What?

JOE: Donna Silliman. On this trip. What if she got pregnant? She could, you know.

PHILIP: Perhaps even as we speak.

FRANKIE: Philip!

PHILIP: But really is that our problem? (*Beat.*) You're

65

not leading up to a discussion of abortion rights, are you?

JOE: No. (*Laughs.*) No. (*Beat.*) I could if you want.

FRANKIE: That's OK.

(*Pause.* BETTY *and* HENRY *eat.*)

JOE: Look, while I have you all together like this.

FRANKIE: Like what?

PHILIP: He means—so uncomfortable.

BETTY: If we're in the way—

JOE: I just want you all to know that *I* know I'm the Chairman of the Department. So you can relax. (*Beat.*) For better or worse that is the case. And as the Chairman I personally will accept full responsibility for what happens to any of the students. OK? Do you hear me—I accept full responsibility. So the rest of you can relax.

PHILIP: Good for you.

FRANKIE: Thanks.

(*Short pause.*)

HENRY: Baldwin, when he was Chairman, would never have had the guts to say that.

(BETTY *sighs and turns away.*)

What? What did I say?

(*Awkward pause as they try to eat and drink their tea crammed together like this.*)

JOE: (*Who has been hiding his face in the box full of tickets*) Who's going to keep the tickets? If they're left with me they're sure to end up lost.

(*He laughs. No one else does.*)

SCENE 5

Projection: WATERLOO BRIDGE

JOE TAYLOR *and* HENRY MCNEIL, *as they walk back across the bridge from the National Theatre. Late afternoon.*

JOE: Let's stop here. Wait for them to catch up. (*Beat.*) It's just drizzling.

HENRY: I didn't even notice.

(*Short pause.* JOE *looks back.* HENRY *looks back.*)

They're taking pictures.

(*Beat.*)

JOE: It was a wonderful performance, didn't you think? (*Laughs to himself.*) The English have such a delicious sense of humour.

HENRY: Very well put. (*Beat.*) When he hid under the table—

JOE: You heard me laughing?

HENRY: I think I was laughing even louder.

JOE: That I very much doubt.

(*He laughs. Short pause.*)

The butler was excellent. He never changed his expression.

HENRY: A very good actor.

(*Short pause.*)

JOE: We could keep . . . (*Nods ahead.*) If you want.

HENRY: I don't mind waiting.

(*Short pause.*)

JOE: Quite the view.

(HENRY *nods. Beat.*).

HENRY: Though I think it's even more impressive from the National's side.

(*Short pause.*)

JOE: (*Suddenly turns to* HENRY) While I have you like—

HENRY: (*Who has turned at the same time, and speaks at the same time*) Joe, I just want to—

(*They both stop. They laugh.*)

Go ahead.

JOE: No, no. Please.

(*Beat.*)

HENRY: I only wanted to say that—. I want to apologize for the way Betty's been acting.

JOE: Why? How has she been—?

HENRY: I don't know what's gotten into her. I've told her I think she's being quite a drag on the whole—

JOE: Henry, she's—

HENRY: Why, I don't know. Maybe it's the pressure about the job. I try to tell her things do work out. (*Laughs.*) But—. (*Smiles and shrugs.*) Maybe she's just a little homesick.

JOE: Maybe.

(*Beat.*)

HENRY: When this whole trip is over I'm sure she'll realize what a good time she had.

JOE: Of course she will. (*Short pause.*) Quite the view.

69

(*Beat.*) Sometimes I think it all looks like a postcard. That I'm inside a postcard. You ever feel that way?

(*Turns and faces* HENRY, *puts his hands on his shoulders.*)

HENRY: A lot.

(JOE *smiles and nods and begins to turn back.*)

So what were you—? You were going to say something. (*Beat.*) You started—

JOE: Henry . . . (*Beat.*) Look, I have no right to ask you for a favour.

HENRY: What are you talking about? You can say this with all the favours you have done me?

JOE: I've done nothing. (*Beat.*) You paid your own way here. What you do with your time—

HENRY: Ask me the favour, Joe. Ask me!

JOE: Promise me, if you don't want to—

HENRY: Ask, for Christ's sake.

(*Short pause.*)

JOE: (*Turns and looks over the Thames.*) Philip is staying behind tomorrow. To wait for Donna Silliman. (*Beat.*) The Amherst class is due to check back into their hotel by two tomorrow. We think it's a fair guess that Donna will be at ours around the same time.

HENRY: So Phil's going to be waiting for her at the hotel. I think that is a very good idea. I support this, Joe.

JOE: Good. (*Beat.*) I'm pleased you agree. I am. I need your support.

HENRY: You can always count on that.

JOE: I know. I do.

(*Short pause.*)

But that wasn't the favour, Henry. (*Beat.*) Phil, I think, should have some company while he's waiting.

HENRY: And that's what you want me to do.

JOE: I have no right to ask this.

HENRY: You have every right. Donna's been one of my students. I have a responsibility here as well.

JOE: That's very very generous, Henry.

HENRY: Bull. It's what anyone would do. So—it's settled. I'll stay behind. Have you talked to Phil about this?

JOE: He suggested it.

HENRY: I'm flattered.

JOE: He wanted company. (*Beat.*) He wanted your company.

HENRY: Who likes to be alone? Should we keep our hotel rooms for the day?

JOE: No. I don't want this costing you anything. You can wait in the lobby. And the second she shows up, you and Phil bring Donna to Stratford.

HENRY: By train?

JOE: I suppose so. I leave that up to you. Maybe there's a bus. I don't know. (*Beat.*) Henry, you do this and I think the Department will owe you at least a dinner.

HENRY: I don't expect anything.

JOE: And we'll make sure Betty's—

HENRY: She won't give you any trouble.

JOE: I meant, we'll look after her.

(*Short pause.*)

Beautiful night. The rain makes it very impressionistic. (*Beat.*) I wonder how much a sign like that cost.

HENRY: Just the electricity. The number of flashing bulbs.

JOE: The National Theatre really must have money.

HENRY: (*Looks back*) They're coming now.

JOE: (*Ignoring him, recites:*)

72

This City now doth, like a garment, wear
The beauty of the morning; silent, bare,
   Ships, towers, domes, theatres, and temples lie
   Open unto the fields, and to the sky . . .

(*Beat.*)

HENRY: Wrong bridge.

JOE: Yes. I know.

HENRY: I didn't mean to—

JOE: (*Ignoring him*) The last time I was on this trip, I
tried to get Baldwin to get a group, students, some of
the teachers, whoever wanted to, nothing formal,
and we'd all get up very early and go to Westminster
Bridge, and just as the sun began to rise, we'd read—

HENRY: That poem.

JOE: (*Turns to Henry*) Just how Wordsworth wrote it.
But Baldwin said who the hell would get up at dawn.

HENRY: He's wrong. I would. (*Beat.*) Maybe when we
get back to London—

JOE: You think others would come?

(BETTY MCNEIL *and* FRANKIE LEWIS *enter, both under umbrellas.*)

FRANKIE: (*To* JOE) Aren't you soaked? Here, get under
the umbrella.

(*He does.*)

BETTY: (*To* HENRY) Others would come where? And how much does it cost?

HENRY: It's a surprise. Right, Joe? For when we all get back.

(PHILIP *enters with his camera.*)

FRANKIE: When we get back from where?

JOE: Stratford.

PHILIP: Wait a minute. Let me get one of the four of you.

(*They stop and turn to him.*)

FRANKIE: That's right. Now we go to Stratford.

(*As she finishes her line, flash from the camera.*)

74

ACT TWO

ACT TWO

ACT TWO

SCENE 6

Projection: IN FRONT OF THE ROYAL SHAKESPEARE
THEATRE, STRATFORD UPON AVON

JOE TAYLOR *and an* AMERICAN MAN, *during the interval of the matinee.* JOE *has a rolled-up poster under his arm and eats ice-cream from a cup; the* AMERICAN *smokes a cigarette and looks through a programme.*

AMERICAN: They don't have any pictures of the actors in their costumes. (*Beat.*) Did you notice?

(JOE *shakes his head.*)

A shame. The costumes are terrific.

JOE: Please. (*Beat.*) Please, don't shout.

AMERICAN: He's good. (*Points to a picture.*) Don't you think he's good?

(JOE *eats and nods.*)

What a costume he's got. (*Beat.*) You got a poster. I was thinking of getting one. Which one did you get?

(JOE *hesitates, then shows him.*)

Maybe I'll get that one too.

JOE: There are plenty of other—

AMERICAN: Look here. (*Shows him an advertisement in the programme.*) They seem to have all kinds of shit. (*Reads:*) 'RSC Merchandise'. (*Beat.*) Posters. T-shirts. Records. Here's an RSC shopping bag. RSC address book. The Game of Shakespeare. What do you think that's about?

(JOE *shrugs, looks away.*)

Maybe my niece would like that, she loves Monopoly. She kills me at it. (*Laughs.*) She's ruthless. I wonder what kind of skills this game teaches. (*Beat.*) So what part of the States do you come from?

JOE: I'm British. I'm a naturalized British citizen. (*Beat.*) I tutor at Oxford.

AMERICAN: No kidding. I'm in insurance. (*Beat.*) So for someone like you all this must be pretty old hat.

(JOE *nods without looking at him.*)

Would you believe this was my first time? It is. Every year for years I've been promising myself . . . (*Beat.*) Finally—. Here I am. (*Laughs to himself.*) The thrill of a lifetime. (*Turns to* JOE.) Doesn't eating that stuff make you even colder?

JOE: Not if you're English.

(AMERICAN *nods, shrugs, looks at the programme, then up.*)

AMERICAN: Theatre's my hobby, you know. We've got a very successful little theatre back home. The high school lets us use the auditorium. I've seen some so-called professionals that weren't any better, really. (*Laughs to himself.*) Last summer we did Thornton Wilder's *Our Town.* You want to know whose arm they twisted to play the Stage Manager? (*Laughs.*) I wasn't half bad either! (*Beat.*) Nothing like these guys, of course. (*Nods towards the theatre.*) These guys are real pros. I'm not even in their league, let me tell you. I don't even deserve to wipe the sweat off these guys' faces. You know what I mean?

(*He laughs to himself.*)

(FRANKIE *hurries in.*)

FRANKIE: (*As she enters*) It's just the intermission? How long *is* the play?

JOE: They're saying all the words. Every now and then they have to do that. So have they called?

FRANKIE: They're here.

JOE: Here? When? They were supposed to call first.

FRANKIE: They rented a car.

JOE: A car?! I told them to take a train or a bus. I'm not sure we have it in the Department budget to rent a—

FRANKIE: Joe, Donna Silliman wants to talk to you.

JOE: Sure. And I want to talk to her. As soon as this is over, I'll—

79

FRANKIE: Now.

(*Short pause.*)

JOE: Now?? (*Looks towards the theatre.*) But there's still—

FRANKIE: I think you should go.

JOE: In my whole life I've only seen one professional production of—

FRANKIE: I think it is important.

(*He hesitates.*)

JOE: Why? What happened?

FRANKIE: She's in my room. Come and talk to her.

JOE: And Phil and Henry?

FRANKIE: They went off sight-seeing. Since they missed the start of the play.

(JOE *hesitates, then goes back to the* AMERICAN.)

JOE: My programme, could I have it back, please? I have to leave.

AMERICAN: Sneaking out?

JOE: No, I am not 'sneaking out'.

AMERICAN: They do go on and on—

JOE: I am not sneaking out!

AMERICAN: (*Handing the programme to him*) I'm not sure I would have paid a pound for that.

JOE: And now there is no need, is there?

(JOE *turns and goes off with* FRANKIE.)

ANNOUNCEMENT: Ladies and gentlemen, will you please take your seats. The performance is about to begin.

(*The* AMERICAN *puts out his cigarette and goes off towards the theatre.*)

SCENE 7

Projection: TRINITY CHURCH GARDEN, STRATFORD UPON AVON

A garden bench. HENRY MCNEIL *and* PHILIP BROWN *sit;* PHILIP *holds a piece of paper. A large book is next to* HENRY.

PHILIP: (*Referring to the paper*) I tell you they cheated us. And I'm not saying that because we only had the car for a few hours. I knew we had to pay for the full day.

HENRY: I can't believe they would—

81

PHILIP: Why not? (*Beat.*) Because William Shakespeare lived here? Wise up, Henry. (*Beat.*) What insurance did you agree to?

HENRY: I don't know. Whatever—

PHILIP: You don't know. So first, without even asking, they stick us for the maximum insurance.

HENRY: How do you know that's the maximum?

PHILIP: Because why wouldn't they?

(*Beat.*)

HENRY: If it was up to me to ask for less insurance then it's our fault.

PHILIP: He saw we were in a hurry. So he took advantage. Did you add this up? (*Beat.*) I just did. Add it up. (*Hands the paper to* HENRY.) Are you adding it up?

HENRY: Yeh.

(*Short pause.*)

OK.

(*He hands the paper back.*)

PHILIP: Now what excuses are you going to make for them?

HENRY: So they overcharged us by five pounds, big deal.

PHILIP: Five pounds *is* a big deal to a lot of people, Henry.

HENRY: They made a mistake. I doubt if they'd bother to cheat someone for five pounds.

PHILIP: Five pounds is five pounds! Five pounds adds up! First thing in the morning I'm going down there and get that five pounds back.

HENRY: Do what you want. If it'll make you happy.

PHILIP: It's not my five pounds. It's the Department's five pounds. (*Beat.*) And you're coming with me.

HENRY: I'm not going to act like that for five pounds.

PHILIP: You mean like you've been cheated? You have been cheated, Henry.

HENRY: Spend half a day to get back five pounds? Who's being foolish now?

PHILIP: It's the principle, Henry!

HENRY: You'll embarrass yourself!!

PHILIP: Have some guts, will you?!!!

(HENRY *turns away. Pause.*)

OK. Sorry. (*Pats* HENRY *on the leg.*) Sorry. I didn't mean . . . Hey, I guess we're just different people, that's all.

(HENRY *turns back to him, nods and then smiles.*)

(*Folding up the bill*) Forty-nine pounds for three hours. Fuck.

(*He puts the bill in his pocket. Short pause.*)

HENRY: You should have been the one to choose the insurance.

PHILIP: You did fine. You did.

(*Short pause.* HENRY *picks up the large book—it is* The Collected Works of William Shakespeare—*and begins to thumb through it.*)

HENRY: (*Without looking up*) Joe got the message, I hope.

PHILIP: He must have.

HENRY: (*Looks at his watch.*) We said five thirty. It's almost six.

PHILIP: (*Shrugs.*) Maybe the idea didn't interest him.

HENRY: It was his idea. In London he was the one who suggested we do this.

(*Beat.*)

PHILIP: Well, I think we should have started when we had at least the four of us.

ACT TWO

(BETTY MCNEIL *enters from the direction of the church. She carries a small bag.*)

BETTY: No Joe?

(*They shake their heads.*)

PHILIP: (*Standing*) Sit down. I dried the bench with my handkerchief.

BETTY: No, Phil, don't—

PHILIP: Please, I've been sitting and driving all afternoon.

HENRY: (*Suddenly standing*) So have I. (*Offering his seat*) Please—

BETTY: I don't want to sit.

(*They are all standing now.*)

HENRY: (*Nods towards her bag.*) What'd you get?

(*She opens the bag and takes out some postcards.*)

BETTY: They were thirty pence each. But I figure since it's going to a church.

PHILIP: Thirty pence?!

(*He shakes his head in disgust. Short pause.*)

It's the same in the States though. Ever been to the gift shop at say the Statue of Liberty? They rip you off there too.

(*Pause.*)

HENRY: (*Having looked at the cards, now hands them back.*) They're nice. You should have bought more.

(*Short pause.*)

BETTY: I thought this idea to read the poem was Joe's.

PHILIP: We were just commenting on that.

(*Short pause.*)

So how was the play this afternoon? It broke my heart to miss it, you know.

BETTY: I think two Shakespeares in one day is asking for trouble. But the kids seemed to follow this one. But we'll see what they're like after tonight. (*Beat.*) It was three and a half hours long.

PHILIP: But I'll bet it seemed like an hour, right?

(PHILIP *turns to* HENRY *and laughs.* HENRY *laughs lightly.*)

BETTY: Why is that funny?

(FRANKIE LEWIS *hurries in.*)

FRANKIE: Joe said to go on without him.

(Left to right): Nathan Lane as Henry, Colin Stinton as Joe and John Bedford Lloyd as Philip in the 1990 Broadway production at the Lincoln Center Theatre at the Vivian Beaumont. Photo by Martha Swope Associates/Carol Rosegg.

(Left to right): Kate Burton as Betty, Nathan Lane as Henry, Colin Stinton as Joe and Frances Conroy as Frankie. Photo by Martha Swope Associates/Carol Rosegg.

(Left to right): Cara Buono as Katie, Elisabeth Shue as Donna and Colin Stinton as Joe. Photo by Martha Swope Associates/Carol Rosegg.

(Left to right): Frances Conroy, John Bedford Lloyd, Kate Burton, Nathan Lane, Cara Buono and Colin Stinton. Photo by Martha Swope Associates/ Carol Rosegg.

PHILIP: What's the matter?

HENRY: What's going on?

FRANKIE: Donna Silliman is . . . She's pretty hysterical actually. I have to go back.

PHILIP: Wait a minute. (*To* HENRY) She was fine in the car, wasn't she?

HENRY: Fine.

PHILIP: What's she saying?

FRANKIE: Henry, Joe would like you to drop by the hotel before the play. Just for a second.

HENRY: Sure. I can go now if—

PHILIP: Hey, if you're going then—

FRANKIE: Stay. He just needs a minute. There's plenty of time. (*Beat.*) He's trying not to make this into a big thing.

HENRY: Make what into a big thing—?

BETTY: What happened?

PHILIP: (*Trying to take* FRANKIE's *hand*) Frankie, are you OK? You look—

FRANKIE: (*Pulls her hand away.*) I'm great. I'm feeling just great, Philip. (*Beat.*) How are you feeling? (*Beat. Turns to go.*) Please just read the poem . . .

(She hesitates, then hurries off. Pause. They look at each other.)

PHILIP: And I thought we were finished with Donna Silliman for the day, but I guess not.

(Short pause.)

I wonder what Joe wants to see us about.

BETTY: Henry. He wants to see Henry.

(Short pause.)

HENRY: We better start if I'm going to see Joe before the show. *(Beat.)* Who wants to begin? *(Beat.)* How about Betty?

(No response.)

Betty?

(He holds out the book to her, after a moment she takes it. And begins to read.)

BETTY: 'To the Memory of My Beloved, The Author, Mr William Shakespeare: and what he hath left us.'
To draw no envy (Shakespeare) on thy name
   Am I thus ample to thy Booke, and Fame;
While I confesse thy writings to be such,
   As neither Man, nor Muse, can praise too much.
'Tis true, and all mens suffrage. But these wayes
   Were not the paths I meant unto thy praise:
For seeliest Ignorance on these may light,

88

Which, when it sounds at best, but eccho's
   right . . .

(*She hands the book to* HENRY.)

HENRY: (*Reads*)
   Or blinde Affection, which doth ne're advance
      The truth, but gropes, and urgeth all by chance;
   Or crafty Malice, might pretend this praise,
      And thinke to ruine, where it seem'd to raise.
   These are, as some infamous Baud, or Whore,
      Should praise a Matron. What could hurt her
         more?
   But thou art proofe against them, and indeed
      Above th' ill fortune of them, or the need . . .

(*He hands the book to* PHILIP.)

PHILIP: (*Reads*)
   These are, as some infamous Baud, or Whore,—

HENRY: I read that. (*Points to spot.*) We're here.

PHILIP: (*Reads*)
   I therefore will begin. Soule of the Age!
      The applause! delight! the wonder of our Stage!
   My Shakespeare, rise; I will not lodge thee by
      Chaucer, or Spenser, or bid Beaumont lye
   A little further, to make thee a roome:
      Thou art a Moniment, without a tombe . . .

89

SCENE 8

Projection: BAR OF THE ARDEN HOTEL, STRATFORD UPON AVON

Night. The bar is closed. JOE TAYLOR *sits at a table with* KATIE TAYLOR *and* DONNA SILLIMAN. *They are laughing.*

JOE: (*To* DONNA) Sounds like his theatre class was studying Harrods a lot more closely than they were the Royal Shakespeare Company.

(*He laughs.*)

DONNA: I think they were. (*Beat.*) Looking at the kids, some of the kids and the clothes they were wearing, I think a basic knowledge of Harrods may have been a prerequisite for the class.

JOE: Yeh. (*Laughs.*) What a waste of money. I don't know, maybe I'm old-fashioned but here is this opportunity—. It's like a living education. That's what England could be. I think that's what our course tries to realize. (*Beat.*) I don't know if we succeed.

(*No response.*)

We try. (*Beat.*) I think we come quite close to succeeding.

(*Beat.*)

DONNA: Sure. You mind if I—?

(*She takes out a packet of cigarettes from her purse.*
JOE *shakes his head.*)

Katie?

(*She offers her one.*)

KATIE: Thanks.

(*She takes one.* JOE *looks at her.*)

For Christ's sake, it's a cigarette!

DONNA: Every week they had three days off to do what
they wanted. No classes or anything.

KATIE: For travel?

DONNA: For farting around. That's how I met Chip.
(*Beat.*) He was bored. He'd *bought* a ticket to one of
the plays we were seeing. (*Beat.*) Do you believe that?

(KATIE *shakes her head.*)

JOE: Why is that so—?

DONNA: On his own he bought a ticket!

JOE: I don't find that—

DONNA: He could have done anything. But he went to
see this play. (*Beat.*) You'd really like him, Professor
Taylor. He's a very good student. Reads a lot. Likes to
go to bookstores. (*Beat.*) He wants to teach. (*Beat.*) We
were walking out of the theatre and he sort of tapped

me on the shoulder and asked for a light. (*Smokes.*) I asked where he was from. He asked where I was from. You're in a foreign country, it's nice to see someone from home. (*Beat.*) It makes you feel relaxed.

KATIE: I feel the same way. I've met two, three Americans on this trip.

DONNA: They're not—. I don't know, critical.

KATIE: They see the same things you see.

DONNA: That's it. Exactly. (*Beat.*) Though there's always . . . (*Laughs.*) One afternoon last week I went with Chip and his class on a quote unquote walking tour of Kensington. The teacher got everyone to count Rolls-Royces. Unbelievable.

KATIE: You're kidding!

JOE: I'm sure there was—

DONNA: I'll bet I know more about the English theatre than his teachers do.

JOE: Donna, you—

DONNA: OK, I missed a few plays. OK, I missed a few classes. (*Beat.*) OK, I missed a lot of plays and a lot of classes, but I'll tell you what, I'm going to see everything we see for the rest of the time we're here.

JOE: We go home in six days, Donna.

DONNA: In those six days, then.

(*Short pause. She smokes.*)

Chip's now gone to Paris. (*Beat.*) His girlfriend made him go. It was either me or Paris. So I was really upset. That's why that stuff in the car—. (*Beat.*) I didn't need that.

JOE: No.

KATIE: No one does.

DONNA: I was vulnerable.

JOE: We understand.

DONNA: He scared me. Professor Brown scared the hell out of me.

(*Beat.*)

JOE: Talk about it as much as you want.

(*Long pause.* DONNA *rubs her eyes and almost cries.*)

DONNA: (*Suddenly turns.*) You're not going to get Chip into trouble? It wasn't his fault. I forgot about Stratford. (*Beat.*) Chip's not his real name, you know.

JOE: As we said at dinner, if you're willing to forget about it, Donna, we're willing to. (*Beat.*) At dinner you seemed to be willing to.

DONNA: I am. (*Beat.*) But what Professor Brown did—. Nothing like that ever happened to me—

JOE: A misunderstanding.

DONNA: How do you misunderstand—?

JOE: (*Turns to* KATIE.) I thought this was over. We had dinner. We talked about this.

DONNA: And my parents? You'll talk to my parents?!

JOE: Why do you assume that? (*Beat.*) We have six more days. They can be lovely days, Donna. But that will be mostly up to you.

(*Short pause.*)

I'm not trying to treat this lightly. I don't want you saying that's what I did. If there's more you want to say? (*Beat.*) We can stay up all night if you like. I don't want you to be unhappy with the way I have handled what's happened. (*Beat.*) What you say has happened.

DONNA: You do think I'm lying—

JOE: I don't want you to get home and start complaining! I don't want you saying—. Look, Katie's been here. She's heard everything.

KATIE: Is that why you wanted me here?

(*Pause.*)

JOE: We know his name isn't Chip. We know his name.

(*Short pause.*)

(*Looks at his watch.*) The play's over. Maybe you and Katie would like to—

KATIE: The rest of the class was going to a restaurant. I know which one.

(KATIE *hesitates, then gets up.* PHILIP BROWN *and* HENRY McNEIL *enter.*)

HENRY: Joe, you missed the whole play. I thought *Antony and*—

JOE: We got talking. (*To* DONNA) We finished, right? (*Beat.*) Right?

DONNA: (*Stands.*) I think we should go.

JOE: Donna, before you do. (*Beat.*) I think if for no other reason than for my sake, you should say what you recall happened in the car. To Professor Brown. (*Beat.*) To his face. (*To* PHILIP) I don't want you saying I put words in her mouth.

PHILIP: What's this about?

JOE: Phil, please. (*Beat.*) Donna.

DONNA: (*After a long sigh*) I told Professor Taylor what you tried to do to me in the car on our way up here.

(*Short pause.*)

PHILIP: Which was??

95

DONNA: That you tried to touch me. In fact, he did touch my breast. Actually he grabbed it. I had to push him away.

PHILIP: Joe, this is—

JOE: Wait. (*Beat.*) Donna. Is there anything else you wish to tell me? Anything at all?

(*She shakes her head.*)

You're satisfied that you've had an honest hearing? (*Beat.*) Then you can go.

(KATIE *and* DONNA *start to go.*)

Katie?

KATIE: What, Dad?

JOE: You have money?

KATIE: Yes.

JOE: Buy her what she wants.

(KATIE *and* DONNA *leave. Pause.*)

Sorry that the bar's closed.

PHILIP: (*Stunned*) You don't believe that girl.

HENRY: She's lying, isn't she?

96

PHILIP: Of course. (*Laughs to himself.*) Why would I—? How could I—? (*Beat.*) Henry was in the car the whole time.

HENRY: Except for about three minutes when I went into a gas station for directions. I already told Joe this.

PHILIP: You already . . . ? You knew about this? When did Donna—?

JOE: As soon as you got here. I talked to Henry before the show.

PHILIP: (*To* HENRY) So throughout the play—

HENRY: Joe made me promise not to say anything. He wanted to get to the truth first. (*Beat.*) And I think that was the right decision, Joe.

PHILIP: But you told Betty?

HENRY: I've always made it clear, you tell me something, you are telling her something. I do not keep secrets from her.

PHILIP: (*To* JOE) He tells Betty. (*Beat.*) And it wasn't three minutes in that gas station! It was more like thirty, forty seconds, Henry.

(*Short pause.*)

Anyway, I didn't do anything. Why would I do something like that? What am I crazy, Joe?

(*Long pause.*)

JOE: I don't think she's going to make a fuss. She was as scared about being yelled at for staying out and missing the bus here . . . (*Beat.*) Katie and I took her out for dinner this evening. That's why I missed the play. I figured something had to be done.

PHILIP: To bribe her you mean?

JOE: She's quite relaxed about it all now, I think. You saw her. (*Beat.*) A few hours ago . . .. Sit down, Phil.

(PHILIP *hesitates, then sits.*)

HENRY: Betty's waiting in the lobby. She wants to take a walk. After sitting all day in the theatre—. (*Beat.*) It's hardly even drizzling any more.

JOE: Good.

(HENRY *hesitates, then leaves.*)

God, what an evening!

PHILIP: What I do not understand is: are you saying you believe this girl.

JOE: No. (*Beat.*) Of course not.

PHILIP: Thank you. Thank you.

JOE: Frankie called the Dean—

PHILIP: The Dean? Frankie? She also knew?

JOE: She's the one who got me. As a woman I think Donna—

PHILIP: Bullshit!!

JOE: As a woman I think Donna found it easier to talk to her. Initially. Then I came into the picture. As the Chairman of the Department.

PHILIP: What did the Dean say?

JOE: Donna's been having a lot of trouble of late. She's close to failing. This course—if we decided to flunk her . . . (*Beat.*) I promised her we wouldn't by the way.

PHILIP: Another bribe?

JOE: I just didn't think it was right. A whole academic career should not come down to a course like—. I mean, you can't force someone to go to the theatre. (*He laughs. Beat.*) The Dean respects you, Phil. (*Beat.*) Not once did he suggest anything but respect for you. He said that if you denied trying to molest—

PHILIP: (*Stands up.*) Of course I deny it! What am I now, a rapist?!!

(*Short pause; he hesitates then sits down.*)

JOE: Then when you have this sort of thing, where it's one person's word against another's. And there's no proof. And there isn't, Phil. She couldn't show Frankie one scratch or anything. Then it's the Dean's policy to not get involved if he can help it. (*Beat.*) I respect him for that. He said basically that I should ignore the matter as best I could. (*Beat.*) He even said we shouldn't have called. This sort of thing, it's best to keep it—. You know. You see I'm learning my job. (*Smiles.*) Things get so damn complicated. And then there's the fact that we're friends. I wouldn't want people to have accused me of—

PHILIP: You're not the one being accused!!

(*Short pause.*)

Henry's wrong about the three minutes.

JOE: He just wanted to be safe. He didn't want to underestimate.

PHILIP: Fuck. (*Beat.*) One messed-up girl accuses me of pawing her and you, Henry, Frankie, the Dean, Betty—. Who else did you call? Baldwin?

JOE: Yes.

PHILIP: You called Baldwin? (*Beat.*) You called Baldwin? I don't believe it.

JOE: He said he remembers warning you once about—

PHILIP: About what?!

JOE: Something about a girl, he couldn't remember.

PHILIP: When I was a student!

JOE: Ah. He didn't say that.

100

PHILIP: I was fucked up over this girl. Another student! I wasn't fucking molesting anyone!!!

JOE: I just had to be sure. (*Beat.*) I didn't know what to do. Baldwin suggested I call the Dean. That's where that came from. So blame him, Phil. He said I should protect myself. (*Beat.*) I talked it over with Frankie. She agreed to make the call. I think hearing about it from a woman . . . We didn't want to scare the Dean. (*Beat.*) We thought this was a great idea. I was happy to have her the one who called. (*Beat.*) The Dean could have said—get her on the next plane. Get you on the next plane. He could have said a million things. We didn't know. But now—it's over. There will be no report, nothing. This I have learned. (*Beat.*) Katie, by the way, was here the whole time tonight. Donna can't change her story. Or add to it now. Katie heard everything. This was my idea.

PHILIP: (*Quietly*) But you thought that I could—

JOE: Let's go to a restaurant. I think we can still get a drink in a restaurant. Let me buy you a drink. (*Beat. Not looking at him*) How was the play? You know I felt awful letting my ticket just waste like that. I wish I could have found somebody. There must have been somebody. If I had known I'd have given it to our maid. She'd have been thrilled. A free ticket to *Antony and Cleopatra*. (*Beat.*) I feel bad. You're hurt. I don't want you to be hurt.

PHILIP: You know, Henry probably said three minutes hoping it'd get me into trouble. He's going to need a job soon after all.

JOE: Phil, Henry wouldn't—

PHILIP: I'm joking.

JOE: Don't even joke like that. People don't act that way.

(*Short pause.*)

So—should we go?

PHILIP: I did touch her shoulder. I remember this. She was staring out of the car. I asked her if she needed to go to the bathroom. She said nothing. So I touched her shoulder.

JOE: There's nothing wrong with that. You were trying to get her attention, right?

(*Short pause.*)

Frankie said she'd leave a note at the desk about where she'd be eating. So if we felt like joining her . . . (*Beat.*) Do you feel like joining her? She was a great help with Donna. You should know this. She never let up for a minute. Even more than me she never believed Donna Silliman for a second. She was right there—demanding to know which breast. Everything. She even yelled at her. Right from the beginning, she—. (*Beat.*) She cared, Phil. (*Beat.*) But that shouldn't come as a surprise, because she—

PHILIP: Sleeps with me? Is that what you're going to say? That it took a woman I sleep with to defend me

from attempted rape?!! (*Beat.*) Thanks. Thanks a lot.
That makes me feel a whole lot better.

(*Pause.*)

JOE: No. (*Beat.*) I wasn't going to say . . .

(*Short pause.*)

PHILIP: (*Looks up at* JOE.) You knew about us, didn't
you? You assume everyone knows that sort of thing.
We haven't exactly been subtle about it. I think even
Howard knows.

JOE: Of course I knew. (*Laughs.*) Sure.

(*He didn't know and now* PHILIP *knows this.*)

But what I was *going* to say was . . . Well, she's a
friend. (*Beat.*) That's what I wanted to say. The
other—. That has nothing to do with this, I'm sure.

(*Pause.*)

How was the play? I can't tell you how much I
wanted to see it. Of all the plays to miss. You know
I'm working on an article on *Antony and Cleopatra.*
How often do you get the chance . . .

PHILIP: (*Without looking at him*) There's a matinee
tomorrow. I could take over the class.

JOE: No, no. It's my turn. (*Beat.*) Let me think about it.
(*Beat.*) Anyway, in the fourth act there's a scene. Eros
is putting armour on Antony and Cleopatra's there.

103

(*Beat.*) Well this is—iconographically speaking—*The Arming of Mars*. It's the painting brought to life! This is the point I wish to make. Eros is Cupid. Antony is Mars of course. And Cleopatra, she's even referred to as Venus in the play, you know. (*Beat.*) So my point is, what Shakespeare has done is write a scene and base it on a painting! Structurally then, here is a representation not of life, but of another representation.

SCENE 9

Projection: PIZZA HUT, UNION STREET, STRATFORD UPON AVON

Later that night, FRANKIE LEWIS *at a table;* JOE TAYLOR *is taking off his coat and sitting down.* FRANKIE *has a pizza and a pitcher of beer in front of her.*

JOE: Phil's going to join us. I hope that's OK.

FRANKIE: Of course it's OK. But I think it's supposed to close in—

JOE: He's just taking a short walk.

(*She nods and eats.*)

He wanted a few minutes by himself.

FRANKIE: How's he doing? How'd he take it?

JOE: What was there to take? Everything was settled. Wasn't it?

104

FRANKIE: Still just to be accused of something like . . .

(*She shrugs. Eats.*)

That's got to make you . . . I don't know. (*Beat.*) A little bitch tries to save her butt and almost ruins your career? I mean, in different hands, Joe, something like this—. His heart must have stopped for a few beats. Mine would have. (*Beat.*) The world can start to look pretty scary if you let it.

JOE: Yeh. (*Beat.*) But he must have known that you and I would never . . .

FRANKIE: Once he caught his breath, but before that . . . What a nightmare for him. (*Pours some beer.*) You're sure you don't want—

(*He shakes his head.*)

JOE: Save it for Phil.

(*Short pause.*)

I think taking her out to dinner helped out a lot. Good idea.

FRANKIE: Thanks.

JOE: Once she relaxed.

FRANKIE: Once you said we weren't going to flunk her.

(*He shrugs.*)

The Department I think should pay for—. And not just hers, but your dinner as well, Joe.

(*He shrugs.*)

I'm serious. Did Katie go with you too?

JOE: She was a big help.

FRANKIE: I told you she would be. So then the Department should pay for her dinner as well. It was business, Joe, remember that. (*Beat.*) Keep the receipt.

(*Short pause.*)

How much was dinner?

JOE: We ate at a pub.

(*Short pause.*)

FRANKIE: Henry says they got cheated on the car rental.

JOE: Shit.

FRANKIE: They were in a hurry, so—. He and Phil are going to argue with them tomorrow.

JOE: Good luck.

FRANKIE: They should have kept it until tomorrow. We could have all gone for a drive. Wouldn't have cost any more, except for the mileage.

JOE: They weren't thinking.

FRANKIE: Henry didn't want to park it on the street.

JOE: Oh.

FRANKIE: Makes sense.

(*He nods. Short pause.*)

JOE: How was the play tonight?

FRANKIE: That's right, of all the plays for you to have missed—.

JOE: I'm thinking of seeing the matinee. Phil offered to—

FRANKIE: Do it, you won't regret it.

JOE: What with the article I'm writing—

FRANKIE: You told me. That's why I said of all the plays . . .

JOE: Oh right.

(*Pause.*)

FRANKIE: Joe. I want to say that I think you handled this whole—problem—perfectly. I thought you should hear someone say that.

JOE: Thank you. I appreciate it. (*Beat.*) We try. (*Laughs.*) Thanks, Frankie.

FRANKIE: The worst-case scenario would have been to try and keep it from the School. Better have the Dean think you're too cautious than—. No one likes surprises. You can't be too careful.

JOE: No.

FRANKIE: You've really got to protect yourself, don't you? Even when it's a silly obvious lie like this; it still could have snowballed. That little bitch . . . (*Beat.*) I couldn't have had dinner with her, Joe. I lied when I said since you weren't, then I should be at the play. I couldn't have even sat and looked at her. (*Beat.*) To accuse Phil. A man I—

JOE: (*Interrupts.*) Respect.

FRANKIE: I think we both do. Why not one of us next?

JOE: You can't be too careful, you're right.

FRANKIE: It's frightening.

JOE: Absolutely.

(*Short pause.*)

(*Without looking at her*) We're sure he didn't do what she said he did?

FRANKIE: Joe?? How can you—?

JOE: We're positive?

FRANKIE: He's our friend! He's your best friend!

108

JOE: Who knows anything about their friends?

FRANKIE: That's a sad admission. (*She looks at him.*) What don't you think you know?

(*Finally he turns away and shrugs.*)

JOE: I will have a little of that. (*Pours some beer into a glass.*) What's important is that we have been fair to all sides.

FRANKIE: I can agree with that.

JOE: I'm sure Phil understood what I had to do.

FRANKIE: If he doesn't, he will. Come on, you're already a ten-times better Chairman than Baldwin ever was.

JOE: I agree. (*Laughs to himself.*) He was an asshole. (*Beat.*) He is an asshole.

(*He laughs. She laughs.*)

FRANKIE: It's going to be a pleasure serving under you, sir.

(*She smiles and salutes. He smiles, shrugs, then nods. Pause.*)

By the way, Joe, the other day when you asked why I hadn't answered the door when you had knocked? Late at night? (*Beat.*) Remember that?

JOE: I remember.

109

FRANKIE: I realized later—. (*Beat.*) I'm not that sound a sleeper to sleep through a guy knocking for—. I'll bet you knocked for a while.

JOE: I did.

FRANKIE: Anyway, I realized that I hadn't been in my room at that time. What time was it?

JOE: About four.

FRANKIE: I'd had trouble sleeping. Jet lag, I guess. And so I'd gone out walking. Imagine a woman going out walking say in New York.

(*She laughs.*)

JOE: She wouldn't.

FRANKIE: No. (*Beat.*) So if it ever comes up, why it would I don't know—I was out walking. (*Beat.*) Howard knows I'm not a sound sleeper.

(JOE *looks down.*)

I called Howard today. There's two feet of snow.

JOE: There's always two feet of snow.

FRANKIE: So—nothing's changed. I told him we were having a wonderful time.

JOE: Except for all the girls claiming Phil's trying to rape them.

(*She hesitates, then laughs. He does not laugh.*)

FRANKIE: (*Laughing*) At least we can laugh about it now.

(*Short pause.*)

I also told Howard how you and I had been palling around a lot together. Spending a lot of time—. He liked to hear that.

(FRANKIE *looks at* JOE, *who looks back.* PHILIP BROWN *enters.*)

PHILIP: You're still here.

JOE: They're about to close.

FRANKIE: Sit down. We have a few minutes yet. Here, finish my beer. I'm sure you can use it.

(PHILIP *sits.*)

JOE: How was the walk?

(PHILIP *nods.*)

FRANKIE: Must have been a traumatic night.

PHILIP: I'm fine.

FRANKIE: Joe was saying how well you took—

PHILIP: I just wish to God someone would have just asked me. That's all.

111

JOE: Come on, I did ask—

PHILIP: To be the last person on the goddamn earth to know! You know what that feels like?!

FRANKIE: Joe did what he thought was best.

PHILIP: For Joe!

JOE: That's not fair.

FRANKIE: He's just learning his job.

JOE: Don't apologize for me. A minute ago—

PHILIP: He still has a lot to learn about how to treat people.

FRANKIE: He's sorry, Phil.

JOE: I'm not! (*Beat.*) How the hell did I know you didn't try to fuck her?!!

(*Short pause.*)

I know now of course. (*Beat. Whispers*) I wished to avoid accusing you. I was trying to do what was right.

FRANKIE: He was, Phil. That's what Joe was trying to do.

(*Short pause.* PHILIP *takes the crust left from* FRANKIE's *pizza and eats.*)

JOE: Frankie called Howard today.

(PHILIP *looks at* FRANKIE.)

There's two feet of snow.

FRANKIE: He sends his best to everyone.

(*Beat.*)

PHILIP: Nice guy, Howard.

JOE: Phil, Frankie was saying that the other night—when I knocked on her door, she *wasn't* asleep. She was out—walking.

PHILIP: Frankie, he knows about—

JOE: I don't know anything!

(FRANKIE *looks to* PHILIP, *then to* JOE. *Pause.*)

FRANKIE: I don't know about you two but I'm exhausted. How long was that play? (*Beat.*) To be honest, I think it was about a week ago that I suddenly started to feel that if I had to see one more play—(*Beat.*) One more three-and-a-half-hour play. (*Beat.*) The fannies the English must have. Tough as leather.

(*Short pause.*)

But that passed. Once I saw the light at the end of the tunnel. Once I had that feeling of being over the hump. (*Laughs.*) Come on, they're closing.

PHILIP: We can finish our beers. (*Beat.*) The play we're seeing on Monday is supposed to be very interesting. I was reading about it.

FRANKIE: Which one is that?

PHILIP: I forget the title. But it's a new play. Very political they say.

JOE: That'll be fascinating. That's very English.

FRANKIE: True.

(*Beat.*)

JOE: In the tradition of Shaw.

PHILIP: Please God, don't let it be that!

(*He laughs;* FRANKIE *laughs; then* JOE *laughs lightly.*)

JOE: (*After a big yawn*) I don't know about you but I'm ready to go home.

SCENE 10

Projection: WESTMINSTER BRIDGE

Early morning. It is raining, cold and windy. HENRY MCNEIL, FRANKIE LEWIS, BETTY MCNEIL, PHILIP BROWN *and* KATIE TAYLOR *have come with* JOE TAYLOR *to Westminster Bridge. They all hold a single piece*

114

of paper. JOE *reads from a book of poetry by Words-*
worth.

JOE: (*Reading*)
   This City now doth like a garment wear
   The beauty of the morning; silent, bare,
     Ships, towers, domes, theatres, and temples lie
     Open unto the fields, and to the sky;
   All bright and glittering in the smokeless air.
   Never did sun more beautifully steep
     In his first splendour valley, rock or hill;
   Ne'er saw I, never felt, a calm so deep!
     The river glideth at his own sweet will;
   Dear God! the very houses seem asleep;
     And all that mighty heart is lying still!

(*He slowly closes the book. In the near distance, Big
Ben begins to strike six. No one looks at anyone else;
six people alone in their own thoughts. One wipes the
rain off his face, one puts up an umbrella but then
takes it down—it is too windy; a portrait of loneli-
ness. When the clock finishes,* JOE *opens his single
piece of paper, and everyone—following* JOE's *lead—
begins to sing quietly, so as not to embarrass themselves (and of course in their American accents).*)

EVERYONE: (*Singing*)
     God save our gracious Queen
     Long live our noble Queen,
       God save the Queen!
     Send her victorious,
     Happy and glorious,
     Long to reign over us,
       God save the Queen!

(JOE *starts the second stanza, others follow, though with a little more difficulty.*)

> O Lord our God, arise
> Scatter her enemies,
> And make them fall.
> Confound their politics,
> Frustrate their knavish tricks,
> On Thee our hearts we fix,
> God save us all!

(*Pause.*)

JOE: Third stanza.

(*He looks down at the paper.*)

SCENE 11

Projection: LUIGI'S RESTAURANT, COVENT GARDEN

The same restaurant as in the first scene, though a larger table. Towards the end of their meal: JOE TAY-LOR, HENRY *and* BETTY MCNEIL, FRANKIE LEWIS, PHILIP BROWN, KATIE TAYLOR, ORSON *and* HARRIET BALDWIN, *and* JOANNE SMITH.

FRANKIE: It will be nice to get home.

JOE: Back to the real world. Back to work!

(*He laughs to himself.*)

PHILIP: Don't remind me. Now we have all those journals to read. (*Beat.*) Orson, not only do we have to see the plays, but then we have to read what our students thought about them.

ORSON: I know the system.

HENRY: Phil, I enjoy reading what my students—

PHILIP: I'm kidding, Henry.

(*He looks at* HENRY *who looks away.*)

FRANKIE: It has been a great time.

JOE: I think we've all enjoyed ourselves.

(*Pause. They eat.*)

HARRIET: Has everyone tried to pack? I remember— when was that, dear?

ORSON: I don't know what the hell you're talking about.

HARRIET: Yes you do. (*Beat.*) I don't remember the year, but—our things didn't fit. We had to buy a whole new suitcase at the very last minute.

(*She laughs.*)

ORSON: The suitcase broke. We bought a new one because it had broken.

HARRIET: That was another year.

ORSON: (*Shaking his head*) Oh forget it. What does it matter? So we bought a suitcase. Who cares?

(*He drinks from his wineglass. Short pause.*)

HARRIET: (*To the others*) It's those Martinis.

ORSON: It is not those Martinis!

(*Short pause.*)

FRANKIE: (*To* HENRY *and* BETTY) You never did get down to their home in East Sussex, did you? (*Beat.*) It's very beautiful. Historic, I should say.

JOANNE: (*To* ORSON) You must be very pleased.

BETTY: (*To* FRANKIE) We were never invited.

(*Beat.*)

HARRIET: You weren't—. Oh, I'm terribly—. You weren't waiting for a formal—?

(*Beat.*)

BETTY: No. We weren't waiting for anything formal. (*Beat.*) I suppose there was just so much we wanted to do. And the time just vanished.

(*Short pause.*)

HENRY: Well *we've* packed everything. Except what we'll use tonight. (*Beat.*) Everything fits. We tried to restrain ourselves—

118

(*He laughs.*)

BETTY: The trip cost us enough as it was.

(*Pause.*)

JOE: I suspect tomorrow morning will be a real mad-house. How did *you* handle it, Orson? Some of the students say they'll take the tube to the airport.

FRANKIE: But the luggage some of them now have.

JOE: That's what I'm saying. And half of them I'm sure are down to their last 50p.

ORSON: That's their problem.

(*Beat.*)

PHILIP: Orson's right. Let them find their own way. It's good training.

(*Short pause.*)

FRANKIE: What time are we supposed to meet?

JOE: In the lobby at eight. No later than eight.

PHILIP: We better say seven thirty.

(*Pause.*)

FRANKIE: (*To* JOANNE) We're really sorry we didn't get the chance to meet your husband, Joanne. It's funny, in the beginning it seemed like there was going to be so much time—

PHILIP: Where did the time go?

(JOE *looks at* PHILIP, *then at* FRANKIE. PHILIP *turns away.*)

JOANNE: He's hoping maybe next year.

(*No one seems to understand.*)

My husband. He's—

ORSON: What does your husband do?

JOANNE: He works in the financial City. (*Beat.*) Near St Paul's.

ORSON: Good for him.

FRANKIE: I love St Paul's.

JOE: (*To* JOANNE) Of course, whenever you're back in the States—

JOANNE: We're talking about a trip—

FRANKIE: We'd love to see you. Both of you.

JOE: Katie would even let her old babysitter have her room, I suppose.

KATIE: I'm never there. I'm in a dorm.

JOE: And why I don't know. (*To* JOANNE) Do you know how much housing is now? Everything's gone crazy. (*Beat.*) But Mary said Katie should have the whole experience of college. I mean, how's she going to have bull sessions with her friends until three in the morning if her parents are right next door? (*Laughs.*) That sort of thing. Right, Katie?

ORSON: (*Eating*) Or how's she going to have boys in her bed when her parents are in the next room?

(*Short awkward pause.*)

KATIE: (*To* ORSON) That didn't stop me in high school.

(*Beat, then laughter.*)

HARRIET: Good for you. Give it back to him.

JOE: By the way, I was reading through Katie's journal this morning—

KATIE: Dad—!

JOE: You let me. I wasn't doing anything you didn't know about. She's got some real interesting things to say about the RSC's *As You Like It.* Very interesting.

PHILIP: Really . . . ?

JOE: You'll have to read it.

HENRY: I'd like to.

JOE: (*To* KATIE) *The Tempest* I think you missed the point of though.

FRANKIE: That's easy enough to do.

HARRIET: Especially at her age.

(*The others nod. Pause. They eat.*)

JOE: What did anyone think of the play last night?

PHILIP: There's a loaded question.

JOE: No. Really. I haven't heard anyone say a word.

ORSON: What was the play last night?

JOE: What was the title? I don't remember. That says something. (*Laughs.*) Some new play, Orson. I wouldn't rush out.

PHILIP: I liked it.

(*Beat.*)

JOE: Good.

(*He shrugs, then laughs.*)

PHILIP: Look, your problem is that you don't think politics belongs in the theatre.

JOE: First, I've never said that. In fact, I have often argued the opposite. Who defends Shaw?

FRANKIE: Please, keep Shaw out of this.

JOE: And second, I happen to believe there is a differ-
ence between politics and sentimental whining.
(*Beat.*) I would kill to see real political thinking on the
stage. Where real problems are really addressed,
Phil. Where I can be engaged! I am not a dumb person. We should not be treated like we were. This is all
I'm saying.

PHILIP: And last night—

JOE: If someone is going to start preaching to me then
he—or she—better have something very very interesting to say. That's all. But to be a captive audience,
forced to listen either to what I already know or what
I know to be a very simplistic, you know, explanation,
then—well, I want to run screaming into the night.
Period.

PHILIP: Bullshit. I repeat, your problem is that you
don't think politics, today's politics, even belong in a
play.

ORSON: Why is that a problem?!!

(*Pause.*)

KATIE: (*Standing.*) Excuse me. Before you get started
again, I promised some of the women I'd join up with
them. It's our last night as well.

JOE: Yes. You told me you'd have to leave early.

HENRY: It was our pleasure to have you, even if for a short time.

HARRIET: She's our godchild, you know.

BETTY: I didn't know.

(KATIE *has opened her purse.*)

JOE: No, no, no! Please, Katie. I'm not that poor. I'm not rich, God knows, but I'm not so poor as that.

KATIE: Thanks Dad. (*Turns to leave.*) Don't stay up too late.

HARRIET: (*Laughing.*) Listen to her.

JOE: Katie, wait a minute. You still have your camera?

KATIE: Yes.

JOE: Come on, of all of us. Come on.

(*He starts moving people together.*)

KATIE: I don't know if there's enough—

JOE: Try. What's to lose? A little closer. (*Beat.*) Of our last night.

KATIE: OK.

(*Everyone is posed.*)

Ready? One. Two. Three.

(*Clicks. Everyone moves.*)

JOE: Another one.

ORSON: No, no. One's enough.

PHILIP: Please, Joe. We're still eating.

JOE: It's probably too dark anyway.

(*He waves* KATIE *off. She leaves.*)

FRANKIE: Thanks, Katie!

HENRY: Thanks!

(*Short pause.*)

JOE: So in this play, we're meant to feel sympathy for miners. Good. Fine. Who doesn't like miners?

ORSON: In my day—

PHILIP: Anyone with a political view you tried to arrest, Orson.

ORSON: Only when it got in the way of—

HARRIET: Please.

JOE: And it gave me goosebumps. This play. Why?

PHILIP: Because it touched—

JOE: Because it pushed obvious buttons! Things in this

125

world are complicated. Not simplistic. You don't help
yourself or anyone else by not recognizing that. By
not using the mind you've got. (*Beat.*) Isn't that what
we teach? Isn't that why we have our students read
what we do—so that they can learn to think? (*Beat.*) A
mind is not a reflex, it is a living thing.

HENRY: The President of the College said that at last
year's graduation.

JOE: I know. And I liked it.

(*Short pause.*)

PHILIP: And I liked the play. So that's that.

FRANKIE: I liked it too.

JOE: Who doesn't like a good cry?

FRANKIE: I learned something about miners.

JOE: You learned what you already believed, Frankie.
Period. (*Beat.*) Trust me, this sort of theatre is old
fashioned. We went through that twenty years ago.
(*Beat.*) You certainly don't find it in the States any
more. (*Beat.*) And in another five, ten years you won't
find it here either. (*Beat.*) I don't want to see it. Americans don't want to see it.

(*Pause.*)

Sorry, I'm dominating the—

PHILIP: We argue like this all the time.

FRANKIE: (*To* ORSON *and* HARRIET) They do. This I can swear to.

ORSON: Nice to see ideas still being discussed in the Department. (*Beat.*) I was afraid after I'd left . . .

(*Beat.*)

JOE: (*Nods towards* PHILIP.) He's fun to argue with. He really is. He never seems to learn, Philip. And I can't help but play devil's advocate. Five kids with arm-bands walking around telling the College to disinvest in South Africa, and you'd think from listening to Phil that it's the sixties all over again.

(*He laughs.*)

PHILIP: Disinvestment has a point.

JOE: Of course it has a point. I don't argue with that. It's your Polyanna-ish hope that is so irritating! It's like he never learns! (*Beat.*) Of course South Africa's bad! Of course!!!

(*Long pause. They eat.*)

BETTY: Professor Baldwin, how is your book coming? Frankie was telling me a little about it.

JOANNE: What is the book about?

HARRIET: Orson is editing the collected letters of Harold Frederic for Cornell University Press.

ORSON: I'm writing the introduction as well.

FRANKIE: That I didn't know.

(*Short pause.*)

JOANNE: I'll be ignorant, who's Harold Frederic?

HENRY: (*Before anyone else can answer*) Nineteenth-century American novelist. Very interesting. Very important.

JOANNE: Never heard of him.

PHILIP: Edmund Wilson liked him.

(*Pause.*)

HARRIET: We've gotten the proofs.

FRANKIE: You're that close?

ORSON: Mmmmmmmmmmmmm.

(*Short pause.*)

Harriet's been helping, haven't you? (*Beat.*) We read them out loud to each other, as we proof. Every night from six to nine. We do about fourteen pages an evening that way. (*Beat.*) Harriet has a lovely voice.

(*Pause.*)

Henry James helped raise money for Frederic's family when he died.

HARRIET: He died drunk. (*Beat.*) He had a drinking problem.

(*Short pause.*)

ORSON: He was a good friend of James. He lived quite a long time in England.

HARRIET: He is said to have called Henry James an effeminate old donkey who lives with a herd of other donkeys around him and insists on being treated as if he were the Pope. (*Beat. To* ORSON) I think I got that right.

ORSON: I doubt if Frederic either said it or felt that way. It is part of the Frederic myth though. (*Beat.*) He had two wives, though only one officially. Two sets of children. One in America, one here. He liked women. They liked him.

HARRIET: Though both families he stuck in the country while he himself went off to carouse in the city.

(*She shakes her head.*)

JOANNE: Sounds very—

ORSON: He wrote *The Damnation of Theron Ware.* Do you know it?

(JOANNE *shakes her head.*)

A very sexy book. (*Beat.*) I reread it all the time.

(*Pause.*)

JOANNE: While I have all of you here, I was wondering if there was anything different or whatever that I could do for next year. If you don't mind I'd like to pick your brains.

PHILIP: I don't know.

HENRY: We had great seats.

JOANNE: I'm sorry I couldn't get any speakers.

FRANKIE: I think it worked out just fine like it did.

JOE: Sometimes a speaker, well, if they don't know the class . . .

JOANNE: I wanted to get an actor.

BETTY: That would have been interesting.

JOANNE: There's a friend of a friend who knows someone who is with the Royal Shakespeare Company.

PHILIP: Really? The students would have loved that.

JOANNE: But he wanted fifty pounds.

PHILIP: For one class? Forget it.

JOANNE: That's what I said. I had thought that they'd do this sort of thing for free.

FRANKIE: I would too.

PHILIP: You'd think they'd want to meet their audience.

JOE: Or just for the publicity.

JOANNE: But if you are interested for next year . . .

JOE: We'd have to put it in the budget.

PHILIP: Absolutely.

JOANNE: Then I guess it was a good thing I didn't tell the guy it was OK.

PHILIP: For next year? He needs to know now?

JOANNE: For this time. He said he needed an answer right then and there.

JOE: That would have been a disaster, really. I think we're what? Quite a lot in the red already. What with the car rental.

FRANKIE: Oh and I said the Department should pay for Joe's dinner in Stratford.

HENRY: With Donna Silliman?

ORSON: Who's Donna Silliman?

BETTY: That girl who said Phil—

ORSON: Oh yes. The Department should pay for that sort of thing. (*Beat.*) Got caught with your pants down, did you, Philip?

131

(He laughs.)

PHILIP: She made it up, Orson.

ORSON: *(Laughing)* I'm sure she did! I'm sure!

(Short pause.)

Henry, I hear you have to move on. All I can say is you shall be missed, dear boy.

HENRY: I don't think that is totally settled as yet. For next year, I mean.

(He looks around. No one looks at him.)

ORSON: Too bad you're not black.

JOE: I don't know about anyone else, but I'm beginning to feel the wine.

ORSON: Yes, we should get another bottle!

FRANKIE: No, no! *(Beat.)* I think I wouldn't mind getting back. I haven't even started to pack.

JOE: I thought you were going to pack this afternoon. What did you do all day if you didn't pack?

(He suddenly turns to PHILIP.)

PHILIP: We should get the check.

JOE: *(Staring at him)* We already have.

ACT TWO

HENRY: Let me see.

(*He takes the bill.*)

PHILIP: I think we should treat Joanne.

FRANKIE: Yes, for all her tireless work.

JOANNE: No, really—

JOE: Out of the Department?

PHILIP: We should split hers.

JOANNE: No, no please, it's I who—

PHILIP: We insist.

JOE: If she wants to pay, Phil.

(*Short pause.*)

JOANNE: I'm serious. Let me pay for myself.

(PHILIP *hesitates, then nods.*)

ORSON: (*To* BETTY) Within twenty-four hours of Henry
James having two strokes, he was calling for a thesau-
rus; the doctor had called his condition paralytic and
he thought there was a more accurate word.
(*Laughs.*) He loved words. I suppose you have to.

HARRIET: Orson.

(*He is quite drunk now.*)

133

I'll pay ours. What did you have, the beef spaghetti?

(*He shrugs.*)

At least one of these four bottles is yours. We'll pay for one whole bottle.

BETTY: Actually, I think he drank—

PHILIP: I'll buy your drinks, Joe. You bought me drinks at the Barbican.

JOE: But only because you bought me drinks at the National. No, no, you don't owe me.

PHILIP: Still, that's OK.

JOE: No. (*Beat.*) Katie didn't have anything to drink, did she? Did anyone notice?

BETTY: She must have. Her glass has been used.

HENRY: Put in something. Don't put in much.

JOE: Let's say seven pounds twenty. What's the VAT on that?

PHILIP: Just estimate, Joe.

BETTY: (*To* HENRY) Here's some money.

JOE: Let me look at that. (*Takes the bill.*) I say we leave no more than 10 per cent. I mean we're leaving tomorrow, right? We're not coming back for a year.

134